pg. 27
28
29
30
56

AMERICA'S PSYCHIC MALIGNANCY
The Problem of Crime, Substance Abuse, Poverty and Welfare—Identifying Causes With Possible Remedies

Publication Number 1086
AMERICAN SERIES
IN
BEHAVIORAL SCIENCE AND LAW

Edited by
RALPH SLOVENKO, B.E., LL.B., M.A., Ph.D.
Professor of Law and Psychiatry
Wayne State University
Law School
Detroit, Michigan

AMERICA'S PSYCHIC MALIGNANCY
The Problem of Crime, Substance Abuse,
Poverty and Welfare—Identifying Causes
With Possible Remedies

By

NORMAN Q. BRILL, M.D.

Professor Emeritus
UCLA School of Medicine
Consultant
VAMC, West Los Angeles

CHARLES C THOMAS • PUBLISHER
Springfield • Illinois • U.S.A.

Published and Distributed Throughout the World by
CHARLES C THOMAS • PUBLISHER
2600 South First Street
Springfield, Illinois 62794-9265

© *1993 by* CHARLES C THOMAS • PUBLISHER

ISBN 0-398-05831-8

Library of Congress Catalog Card Number: 92-32410

With THOMAS BOOKS *careful attention is given to all details of manufacturing and design. It is the Publisher's desire to present books that are satisfactory as to their physical qualities and artistic possibilities and appropriate for their particular use.* THOMAS BOOKS *will be true to those laws of quality that assure a good name and good will.*

Printed in the United States of America
SC-R-3

Library of Congress Cataloging-in-Publication Data

Brill, Norman Q. (Norman Quintus), 1911-
   America's psychic malignancy : the problem of crime, substance
abuse, poverty, and welfare—identifying causes with possible
remedies / by Norman Q. Brill.
     p.   cm.—(American series in behavioral science and law)
   "Publication number 1086"—Ser. t.p.
   Includes bibliographical references.
   ISBN 0-398-05831-8 (cloth)
   1. United States—Social conditions—1980- 2. Social problems.
3. Crime—United States. 4. Poverty—United States. 5. Substance
abuse—United States. I. Title. II. Series.
HN59.2.B75 1993
361.1'0973—dc20   92-32410
                                                                         CIP

FOREWORD

Following World War II, civility in America declined markedly. Its cities became jungles; its schools "blackboard jungles." Dr. Frederick Goodwin, as head of the Alcohol, Drug Abuse and Mental Health Administration, observed, "One could say that as the loss of social structure in this society, and particularly within the high impact inner-city areas, has removed some of the civilizing evolutionary things that we have built up, maybe it isn't just the careless use of the word when people call certain areas of certain cities jungles."

People in America are deprived of their liberty, not by political or religious oppression, but by crime and other lack of civility. The fear of crime strikes at a most fundamental right—the right to feel secure at home and on the streets. It is, actually, the most serious threat to the quality of life of the average citizen. It erodes the viability and vitality of community life, affecting all manner of decisions ranging from the way people regard their neighbors to the way they do business. Massachusetts Governor William Weld expressed a widespread feeling when he said recently, "Unless our families are free to walk the streets in safety, no other freedoms really matter."

Surveys show that Americans are terrified by crime and rank it at the top of their list of concerns. The fear takes its toll on the psyche. It shapes lives. There is hardly an area of life that goes unaffected. It influences the way people travel, work and live.

Precaution against crime has become the touchstone of every aspect of daily life. Phone numbers are unlisted. Bullet-proof shields separate taxi-driver and passenger. Security has top priority in building design. University campuses are monitored by television cameras. The streets are deserted. The ordinary individual, living as though a prisoner, can no longer enjoy even the simple pleasure of a walk. Dwellings are referred to as "a padded cell." Seeking refuge in the suburbs, people abandon (not sell) their homes.

Recent immigrants to the United States, having struggled to get here,

v

are dismayed at what they find. Yearly each of the ten largest U.S. cities has a homicide rate higher than that of "bloody Ulster" in Northern Ireland. During the peak years of the war in Vietnam (1966 to 1972), 44,000 Americans were murdered with handguns on the home front. In a typical year, over 14 million episodes of serious (felonious) crime are reported to law enforcement authorities in the United States, with many million more episodes of minor crime, and with perhaps as many as 21 million additional criminal victimizations that are not formally reported. Put another way, one of every eight people is victimized by crime each year in the United States.

James Q. Wilson has observed: "A young male born today in the city of Detroit and spending his life in the city of Detroit has a greater chance of dying as a result of murder than a combat infantryman had of dying in combat in the Second World War." In Detroit, during a four-month period, 102 youngsters age 16 or under were shot, a number by "stray bullets." Similar statistics are available for New York, Chicago, Atlanta, Miami, and Washington, D.C., the nation's capital.

In a study at the University of Maryland in Baltimore, of 168 teenagers who visited an inner-city clinic for routine medical care, 24 percent had witnessed a murder and 72 percent knew someone who had been shot. It took only a few days after war erupted in the Persian Gulf for nationwide concern to be expressed about its impact on children and on how to handle the stress; physicians reported that patients repeatedly asked for advice on how to respond to the needs of worried children. Yet children in the United States live daily in a state of warfare.

At an anti-crime conference at the Justice Department, President Bush observed: "During the first three days of the ground offensive more Americans were killed in some American cities than at the entire Kuwaiti front. Think of it—one of our brave National Guardsmen may have actually been safer in the midst of the largest armored offensive in history than he would have been on the streets of his own hometown."

Why the crime? There is no dearth of explanation—the demise of the family and religion as socializing forces; inadequate social facilities; poverty; unemployment; racial and class tensions; unequal opportunities; drugs and alcohol; firearms; disrespect for authority; alienation; frustration; boredom; the decline of the role of the male; the glamorization of violence; the culture of consumption; population growth; corruption in public office; heredity; and abnormal chromosomes.

Behavior of any sort is at least partially the result of the values that people internalize. For all its poverty, the streets of Calcutta are safer than those in the United States. Within the confines of the shtetls, the poor Jewish villages that dotted Russia, Poland and other European countries until the early part of the 20th century, the denizens did not have much but they shared and supported each other. Crimes committed for money needed desperately for family food supplies are singularly absent from the criminal docket in the United States. Even in poor communities most people do not rape or rob. As a rule, repeat offenders are criminals out of choice and not out of necessity or unhappy circumstance. The habitual offender is a professional who decides to be a burglar or an armed robber the way one might choose to be a lawyer.

People are motivated both by "internal" sanctions such as guilt and "external" sanctions such as ostracism. Even compliance with criminal law is influenced more by feelings of obligation and by peer disapproval than by the fear of prison. Focusing on the weakening of the "internal" and "external" sanctions that control behavior would explain much of crime. Environmental stimuli can either foster or inhibit aggression. The law is part of those stimuli. With the loss of feelings of obligation and peer disapproval, law enforcement takes on a greater burden.

One immigrant from Poland has this to say, "When I came to America, I learned that this was a country without order. People are free to do as they like. There's no discipline—at home, at school, or anywhere. And the media encourages wild behavior." (The fundamental activity of Americans—watching television—has involved, for the average viewer, seeing 150 acts of violence and 15 murders a week.) "Up yours!" say the young in America. Years ago Sholom Aleichem told the story of Russian immigrants on a ship to America. The father says to his son who is misbehaving, "Wait, you're not in America yet." Since the time of that story, discipline in America has become even more attenuated.

In America, civil rights have been proliferating, but little attention has been paid to civic virtue from which rights derive their surest protection. In a large country blessed with natural resources, little attention has been paid to civic responsibility. The United States has a Bill of Rights but not a Bill of Duties. Yet the expansive talk of individual rights has undermined notions of obligation and community. A conversation in the United States about responsibilities is a rarity. As law professor Mary Ann Glendon puts it, "For most of our history, and even now, we have not had a well-developed public language of responsibility to match our language of rights." And she adds that, because of the heterogeneity of our population, "we have fewer common histories, traditions, religions to bind us together. We look more to the law as a carrier of certain common values."

With the focus on rights, liberty has been turned into license. Columnist John Leo of *U.S. News* writes: "Defining and protecting rights is important in any political culture, but this culture has reached the point where the obsession with individual rights is making it hard for us to think socially, let alone restore the balance between individual and community rights, between personal rights and personal obligations. Rights talk has become so overwhelming that it distorts, co-opts or obliterates issues that are clearly social . . . America is more and more coming to look like a random collection of atomized individuals bristling with rights and choices but with no connectedness or responsibility for one another."

In this book, "America's Psychic Malignancy," Dr. Norman Q. Brill, professor emeritus at the UCLA School of Medicine, argues that much of the problem of crime, poverty, welfare, substance abuse and emotional disorders can be traced to early childhood experiences. Children who are reared in dysfunctional homes, he observes, contribute disproportionately to these problems. He argues that interventions in early life offer the best possible approach to solving the problems that government programs have thus far failed to solve. It would involve preventing, instead of trying to undo, what has already been produced.

Expanded childcare facilities are crucial to the solution, he says, and recognition must be given to the adverse effects of teenagers having children they are incapable of rearing properly. After-school programs are desperately needed for the children who are alone after getting out of school because parents work; they either watch television or get into trouble. For the good of society, he argues for mandatory public service of some kind for high school and college graduates.

Dr. Brill has been interested in the relationship between social class and psychiatric disorders as far back as 1960. At that time the prevailing belief was that poverty caused mental illness despite the fact that not all the poor were ill and rich people also had psychiatric illnesses. In 1969, with the assistance of a sociology graduate student, he studied the extent to which mentally ill hospitalized patients attributed their illnesses to the experience of poverty and later on how their perceptions varied according to their social class. After the introduction of neuropleptics, leading to the wholesale discharge of patients from state hospitals, interest in prevention, which was never great, waned.

It was then that Dr. Brill explored in depth what was known about the role of poverty. What became clear was the relationship between poverty, substance abuse, crime, and societal variables. Looking more deeply into these problems, he found the common denominator was childhood experience. Studies showing that poor adjustment in adult life could be predicted by observing the behavior and home environment of young children seemed to be ignored in government programs.

Protecting individual rights has a higher priority than protecting the rights of society. As a result, there has been a gradual deterioration in behavior, attitudes and quality of life along with an increasing failure of government programs that were supposed to eliminate, or at least reduce, the problems. All of the money and effort directed toward the elimination of poverty, welfare, substance abuse and crime have not been helping and what is seen instead is an increase in family disintegration, interpersonal conflict, emotional disorders, violence and hopelessness.

Dr. Brill has a distinguished career. He is one of the country's most highly regarded teachers and authors in psychiatry. He was trained in neurology, psychiatry and psychoanalysis. He spent over five years in the U.S. Army during World War II. From 1941 to 1944 he was Chief of Psychiatry and Neurology at Fort Bragg and from 1944 to 1946 he was Chief of the Psychiatry Branch and later Deputy Director of the Neuropsychiatry Division of the Surgeon General's Office under Gen. William C. Menninger.

Following World War II, Dr. Brill was Professor and Chairman of the Department of Neurology at Georgetown University School of Medicine and served part time as Chief of the Research Section of the Neuropsychiatry Division of the Department of Medicine and Surgery of the Veterans Administration Central Office assisting in the development of the research program in the V.A. hospitals. In 1953, he was appointed Professor and Chairman of the Department of Psychiatry and Director of the Neuropsychiatric Institute at the new UCLA Medical School and remained as Professor of Psychiatry until he retired (mandatory at age 67) in 1979. After that, he worked as associate chief of staff for education at the Brentwood V.A. Hospital until the fall of 1988, and then served as acting chief of staff. He has served as a consultant to the Surgeon General of the U.S. Army and Air Force and was appointed by President Kennedy to the Board of Regents of the National Library of Medicine, and chairman of the Board, 1964–65. He has also served as President of the Washington Psychiatric Society, the American College of Psychoanalysts, and the Benjamin Rush Society.

This book is born of wisdom and experience.

RALPH SLOVENKO

PREFACE

Increasing crime, substance abuse, homelessness, and poverty not solved by welfare, a persistent hard core, and expanding need for treatment of nervous and mental disorders, along with a population that exhibits and tolerates more and more deviant behavior are symptoms of a serious American disease. There is no current effective cure, although some of the measures that have been adopted have had some beneficial affect. In a sense, it is like the problem of lung cancer. Treatment cures some and provides temporary help for others. But, despite all efforts, the basic problem remains unresolved and there is now increasing emphasis on prevention. If all people stopped smoking, there most assuredly would be less lung cancer—but some cases would still occur.

There is good reason to believe that some of our society's illness can be prevented and some can be helped. It is not a simple thing like smoking that is causing the trouble. It is the unhealthy, traumatic, abusive, neglectful, incompetent, undirected, deficient, upbringing of children that contributes to the development of America's psychic malignancy. A preventive program that includes the early identification of children at risk and provides substitute healthful environments for them will reduce the incidence of socially inadequate or mentally disordered citizens. All of crime and poverty will not be eliminated, but there can be a considerable improvement in the country's social environment along with diminution in the deterioration of the culture than has been going for the past 30 or more years. It will keep America from going down the tubes. It is my intention to examine the problem of crime, substance abuse, poverty and welfare, identify some of their causes and to suggest possible remedies.

NORMAN Q. BRILL, M.D.

CONTENTS

AMERICA'S PSYCHIC MALIGNANCY
The Problem of Crime, Substance Abuse,
Poverty and Welfare—Identifying Causes
With Possible Remedies

Chapter 1

INTRODUCTION

Something has happened to the American dream. In the past, hard work, loyalty, and reliability were trusted to lead to success. Now it may result in being laid off, unemployment and even poverty and welfare. No longer can a person feel assured that his efforts will guarantee security. A feeling of optimism about the future and of American greatness, prosperity, opportunity, fairness, and tolerance has given way in many to pessimism, fear, disillusionment, distrust and anger—and in some to despair and hopelessness.

This change is not one that is just an outgrowth of the current recession, or the low of an economic cycle that has been experienced many times throughout the years. It appears to be the result of a profound change in society that has taken place and promises to persist. Some think of it as our "going down the tubes."

Ernest L. Boyer, President of the Carnegie Foundation for the Advancement of Teaching, in an article "America Has Orphaned Its Young" writes, "It is shocking that such a high number of kindergarten students come to school educationally, socially and emotionally not well prepared. It is unacceptable that some don't know where they live, can't identify colors or are unable to write their full and proper name."

He claims no outside program, no surrogate or substitute arrangement, however well planned or well intended, can replace a supportive family that gives the child human bonding and a rich environment for learning. Once children were born at home with neighbors and midwives in attendance. Family doctors made house calls. Grandparents, aunts, uncles and cousins often stopped by for casual conversation. Neighbors watched over kids and patched up cuts and bruises. The corner grocer kept an eye out for trouble. Pastors, priests, and rabbis ministered at times of joy and grief when parents were anxious or confused. It was necessary to have such a circle of support. Gradually, this protective ring was broken. Neighbors grew more distant, doors were locked, friendliness was replaced by fear. Children were warned to avoid people they did not know.

3

Relatives moved far away. Families became isolated and disconnected, struggling alone, and reaching out to someone without pushing buttons on a telephone. Modern life destabilized former certainties and weakened networks of support.

So many parents have no work, and have virtually no network of support. It is a disgrace that in America today one in every four children under the age of six is growing up in a family that cannot afford safe housing, good nutrition, or quality health care benefits that should be the right of every child.[1]

Stay at home mothers are now rare. According to a California Task Force on the Changing Family, less than one quarter of all Los Angeles households consist of married couples with children. One-third are adults living alone. Slightly less than one-fourth of households are of childless married couples. Eight percent are of co-habitating couples. Eleven percent are headed by a single parent, usually a poor minority woman.

The upheaval in family life is linked to growing poverty, rising school drop-out rates, crises in child and elder care, juvenile crime and drug and alcohol abuse.

Sixty-two percent of American mothers work outside the home. "Many women, combining careers and motherhood, are so stressed out that life is little more than an endurance test." An accountant refers to a client's wife who is at home with children as a luxury item.[2]

At no time in the past 75 years has the United States experienced the amount of crime, poverty, substance abuse, disintegration of the family, out of wedlock births, and homelessness that is currently being experienced. There has been a serious decline in the quality of life now characterized by fear and pessimism while the standard of living for most has improved as a result of technological advances.*

There is an increasing awareness that government (at all levels) is unable to cope with or solve the many problems that now confront America. Prisons are overflowing and criminals are being released prematurely to make room for other criminals. We have a greater proportion of our population in prison than any other western country, a higher percentage of female headed households, more homeless and

---

*Lester Rand, President of the Rand Youth Poll, N.Y., found that car ownership by teens has tripled in the past decade, with 36% of those eligible to drive now owning cars. The number with their own telephone nearly doubled and 47% own TVs compared with 29% in 1980. (Wall Street Journal, May 3, 1990. p. A1.)

more people abusing alcohol and other drugs. Cities are plagued by violent gangs, unsightly graffiti and refuse on the streets and roads.

In a poll conducted in August 1991 for Time/CNN, 68% of New York City residents said the quality of life had grown worse in the past few years; 60% were worried about crime and 45% believed the quality of life would continue to get worse. Fifty-nine percent would live elsewhere if they could. Seventy-three percent felt the city was a dangerous place in which to live and that it was getting tougher. There had been a surge of drugs and violent crime that the government seemed utterly unable to combat. In tougher neighborhoods, teachers train young children to hit the floor at the sound of gunshots. Even the basic rudiments of civil behavior seemed to have evaporated. The streets have become restrooms for people as well as animals. There are more than 100 languages being spoken by children in the city public schools. Less than one-half read at above the first grade level and one-third drop out before their senior year. Almost one-third of the local school boards are under investigation for corruption. By no means is this situation characteristic of only New York. Urban centers throughout the country are faced with comparable difficulties.[3]

As far back as 1980, a Presidential panel looking at the environment found the global outlook extremely bleak. It predicted a world that could become more crowded, more polluted, and more vulnerable to disruption (than the world at that time), and that despite greater material output, the increase in the world's population to 6.5 billion, (from 4 billion in 1975) mostly in poorer, less developed countries, will result in a lack of food for the urban poor, lack of jobs, and increasing illness and misery (that may slow the population increase). Soil salinity will increase and carbon dioxide in the atmosphere and temperature will rise. The panel believed the only solutions were complex and longterm and were linked to the persistent problems of poverty, injustice and social conflict.[4]

Such predictions are not popular. People do not like to hear the truth, which is the case with crime today. It seems too big to cope with — and they hope it will go away.

Alan Cranston, the senior senator from California, reported a spirit of estrangement between the government and the governed. Fifty-eight percent of people interviewed in a Harris poll believe their leaders are out to take advantage of them. Half feel that many of those in power are a little crooked. This and other polls show a growing belief that the political process is so unresponsive and dishonest that it cannot be used by voters for their purpose. Moreover, there is anger among people who feel loss of control over their own lives and manipulated by an insensitive faraway bureaucracy. People are not only turned off by government, they feel it is incapable of solving their problems and is irrelevant to their lives."[5]

When one congressman in California represents 500,000 people and two Senators 30 million, it is no wonder that the average citizen has little prospect of any meaningful access to his elected representatives. It is the special interest groups that contribute money to their campaigns for re-election that are given the attention.

According to Benjamin Bycel, Executive Director of the Los Angeles Ethics Commission, big money and ethics are incompatible. He points out how most campaign funds come not from individual citizens, but from special interests with a strong financial interest in the outcome of the election. These special interests are unlikely to be much concerned with ethical behavior of the incumbent officeholder as long as they have access. So the war chests of incumbents are usually brimming with contributions from people who may have little interest in good government."[6]

With the number of congressmen fixed by law at 435, as the population of the county increases, each congressman and senator will represent more and more people and unless there is some change in the system, the situation will get worse. Now only 50 percent of people bother to vote and it may be less in the future.

The rapidity of changes that have taken place in our society in the past 50 years are astounding and has paralleled the rate of change in the speed of travel, communications, and calculation. Some of the more obvious manifestations of the changes are increased freedom of women and the greater opportunity for self-support that they have, the decline in religious authority, the increased divorce rate, the unparalleled affluence achieved by many young people, the population explosion, the great medical advances, the use of computers, the expanded welfare program, social security and increased emphasis on social planning.

There has also been a tendency to wholesale rejection of traditional authority, of manners, speech, standards of morality and sexual behavior, of dress, and grooming. For many, human rights rather than responsibility have become the more important issue. Insanity is no longer a justification for hospitalization. State hospitals have been closed; mentally ill have been returned to their communities and the public is expected to tolerate deviant behavior that in the past would have resulted in institutionalization or arrest.

Even the treatment approach to the mentally ill has changed. There has been an increasing rejection of a psychoanalytic orientation (that is designed to not only help patients understand the genesis of their illnesses, but to see the role that they themselves play in creating and perpetuating their own problems) in favor of more simplistic (more scientific?) approaches that either rely on medication (based on the theory that there is something chemically or electrically wrong with the brain) or the elimination of current societal stresses.

These new approaches tend to ignore the elements of an individual's behavior that contribute to his illness and tend to place responsibility for the causation, as well as the cure, on society. The patient then tends to be seen as a passive victim and passive recipient of treatment as in the traditional medical model where the physician is expected to provide the cure—be it an operation, a transfusion or a prescription.

There are some who contend that society is at fault when an individual commits a crime because society did not recognize and meet his or her needs and, therefore that no one should be locked up.

There has been a change in attitude toward work that now increasingly must be enjoyable and not just a means of support. In face of a high unemployment rate and a greater percentage of people receiving welfare and other assistance than any time in the past, it is necessary to import foreign workers to do the work that Americans often reject as menial and insufficiently rewarding. It is a far cry from the time that people felt fortunate to have any kind of job. It is probably just a matter of time until adequate income, housing, legal services, clothing, food, recreational facilities and transportation (as well as medical care and education) will be considered entitlements.

We have come a long way from the Protestant Ethic that dominated the American culture for a long time and stressed such things as morality, hard work, buying only that which one could afford, thrift, consideration for others and postponement of immediate gratification for the sake of greater gratification later on.

Compromising opposing views have been replaced by demands, by demonstrations, occupying buildings, blocking streets—by putting one's body on the line (an old Communist tactic). We have been witnessing terrorism, increasing violence and crime, decreasing marriage rates and

increasing divorce rates.* One stays married or just lives with someone else—as long as one enjoys it. There's little thought of working out
differences.

Somehow, and perhaps partly out of a misinterpretation of psychoanalytic investigations, there developed the myth that if children were to
avoid being neurotic, they were not to be frustrated. Parents grew afraid
to cross their children or set limits. Teachers tended to run popularity
contests by being permissive and non-demanding. People seem to have
forgotten that the good parent is not the one who is solely concerned
with winning a child's approval by always giving it what it wants and
sparing it any frustration or denial. Neuroses were to be avoided at all
costs, nothing was to be repressed, and impulses were to be acted on if
one were to be healthy. Now instead of our seeing classical neuroses, we
see character disorders and pathological behavior.

Violence is sanctioned when society merely takes measures to control
it but does not prevent it, and this in itself may well be a contributing
factor in its increase here and throughout the world.

It was claimed that Mao Tse-Tung was able to markedly reduce crime,
prostitution, and drug use in the People's Republic of China by establishing
a philosophy of emphasis on what was best for society and not what was
best for the individual. Even mental illness was regarded as being partly
the result of preoccupation with self rather than concern for society.
This, of course, had a profoundly limiting effect on individual freedom
to do what one pleased; as long as societal goals were paramount, individual wishes had to be secondary. The point of all this is that government
can solve, or at least succeed in providing partial remedies, if it is serious
and determined to do so and has a population that is willing to pay the
price (or cooperate even if not willing). Perhaps it was the idealism and
concern for society that attracted so many young people to Mao's philosophy in the 1960's.

It is difficult to characterize a society that is complex and ever changing,
but certain changes in American culture are quite clear. There has been a
decrease in respect for and submission to authority. Government is no
longer seen as infallible and parents are no longer automatically regarded
as wise or treated with respect. With the increase in communication, via
radio and television, at times instantaneous, people are more knowledge-

---

*At least 40% of marriages in the United States end in divorce. In 1987, one of six children lived
with a single parent family—50% of which had incomes below the poverty level.[6]

able and there is a much more skepticism and distrust of statements and actions of political leaders. To a greater extent than before, people seem to abide only by laws with which they agree. They are more apt to demonstrate against those with which they do not agree.

The British Prime Minister, some years ago when commenting about the Russian's disregard of human rights, was careful not to be too vehement in his disapproval, preferring to compromise morality for practicality. Maybe this is what most politicians are doing, engaging in a continuing compromise with morality for practical reasons and thereby contributing to a gradual erosion of morality and adherence to a philosophy of pragmatism. Is this what many people today are perceiving when they express concern about a creeping immorality?

We have become increasingly hedonistic, not only just in seeking pleasure, but having to have it right away. You ask her for her name later. Drugs of all kinds have been resorted to with increasing frequency to achieve the Utopian existence that so many are seeking and expecting.

Self-denial is not fashionable anymore. If sexual behavior is any indicator of what is going on—every conceivable manner or self-titillation is being explored in the search for the ultimate in joy. An orgasm is not enough. Donald Campbell, in his presidential address to the American Psychological Association, chided his fellow psychologists for siding with self-gratification over self-restraint and for regarding guilt as a neurotic symptom. He complained that modern psychologists not only describe man as selfishly motivated but implicitly or explicitly teach that he ought to be so. His complaint seems to have gone unheeded.[8]

Society is expected to adjust to individuals, not individuals to society. In California, instruction in elementary schools must in some places be given in Spanish. While the reasons for this are obvious, it is a far cry from the expectation years ago, when there were mass migrations of Irish, German, Scandinavian, Italians, and Middle Eastern European Jews to this country, that they had the responsibility to learn the language of the country to which they had come and not vice versa. Now in Los Angeles election ballots are printed in both English and Spanish.

To be sure, the majority of Americans are law-abiding, honest, hardworking citizens who are generous and eager to help others who are less fortunate and are interested in their children's welfare and future. The growing minority of the amoral or criminal element of the population that rejects acceptable standards of behavior and influences the quality of life of the rest of society like a cancer, is, however, an ever present threat to an individual's survival.

The many social changes have been associated with the growing national debt, the increasing annual billion dollar budget deficits, and the crippled banking system. The U.S. economy since about 1973 has been suffering from a slow debilitating disease. Growth in productivity has dropped, the competitiveness of industry has declined, the once steady rise in living standards has faltered and wages have stagnated. Most Americans doubt their children's generation will live as well as they do.[9]

Despite all the changes, the problems, the crime, the unfairness, and the poverty, the United States is still a great country envied for its freedom, its generosity, and its humanity. It is the fear that its greatness is being threatened that prompted this review.

During recessions, attention turns more to domestic problems, and there is rising complaint or objection to our preoccupation with the problems and conflicts in the rest of the world. Politicians respond by proposing programs to deal with the economic and crime problems that are the most disturbing. It is not generally recognized that poverty, welfare, crime, substance abuse and homelessness are inter-related. The causes of these problems are not confronted. If anything is to be done, money is appropriated as the solution, and it ends up with poverty being catered to but not eliminated. Welfare is provided as an entitlement, not as a limited expedient. Harsher penalties or building of more prisons are the proposed answers to crime which is out of control, prosecuting drug dealers and users or legalization of drugs are looked to as the best approach to substance abuse, and emergency provisions for the housing of the homeless is urged for that very complex issue.

In examining the various perspectives of each of these societal dilemmas, it may be possible to identify some of the causes and thereby see the possibility of solutions that hopefully will be in an improvement over what has been utilized so far.

While much of what will be discussed is depressing and upsetting. I remind myself, as counseled by the Annual Thanksgiving Editorial of the Wall Street Journal "that for all our social discord we yet remain the longest enduring society of free men governing themselves without benefit of kings or dictators. Being so, we are the marvel and the mystery of the world, for all that enduring liberty is no less a blessing than the abundance of the earth." It is too painful to witness this great country disintegrate while we continue to use remedies that have already proven to be ineffective.

Dr. Don Flinn was most helpful in the writing of the chapter on Substance Abuse, and I am grateful to him for providing the assistance that I needed in the preparation of this book.

REFERENCES

1. *L.A. Times,* December 8, 1991; p. M5.
2. Beyette, B.: New Minority Mom. *L.A. Times,* December 3, 1989; p. El.
3. Attinger, J.: The Decline of New York. *Time,* September 17, 1990; p. 36.
4. Toward a Troubled 21st Century. *Time,* March 4, 1980.
5. Report to California. 94th Congress, 1st Session, March 1976; No. 32.
6. *L.A. Times,* December 3, 1991; p. B7.
7. McClennan, J. and Trupin, E.: Prevention of Psychiatric Disorders in Children. *Hospital and Community Psychiatry,* June 1989; 40:0. p. 630.
8. Campbell, D.T.: Morals Make a Comeback. *Time,* September 15, 1975; p. 94.
9. Murray, A.: The Outlook. *Wall Street Journal,* December 2, 1991; p. 1.

Chapter 2

THE CRIME PROBLEM*

We are a crime ridden, violent society with overflowing prisons and courts unable to handle all of the cases brought to them. Police acknowledge their inability to maintain a fear-free atmosphere. City people live in homes with barred windows and security systems. Women are afraid to go into elevators or parking structures. Hotel doormen advise people to take cabs instead of walking short distances—to avoid being mugged or robbed. Taxi drivers carry limited amounts of money because of the fear of being held up. Gangs run rampant and randomly shoot people sitting quietly in their homes or standing visiting in the street. Police have to ride buses and street cars in San Francisco and Subways in New York to try to prevent criminals from robbing and assaulting passengers.

The rates of robbery, murder and rape have tripled since 1960. People, especially the elderly, fear to venture from their homes at night—and no longer feel free to just walk around the block. Weapons in the hands of young people exceed anything the U.S. has seen before. Increasingly, psychiatric reports of juvenile killers indicate these juveniles show no feeling or remorse about their crimes that are characterized by viciousness and sadism.

Criminals are being released from jails in order to make room for other criminals. Sometimes it takes years to bring criminals to trial even when millions of people have witnessed the crime on television. In one California city, felons were released without trials because there weren't enough judges to hear the cases.

Police are criticized for taking hours to respond to property crimes and investigating most crimes. Fifty percent of Los Angeles police claim the (criminal justice) system is unsound, with plea bargaining because of

---

*Sir Martin Roth of the University of Newcastle on Tyne at the annual meeting of the American Psychiatric Association in 1971 gave a lecture, "Human Violence as viewed from Psychiatric Clinic." He warned that the psychiatrist who turns his attention to such problems is unlikely to receive a friendly reception—that any approach that is medical will be suspected as biased.

an unmanageable load of cases, (and because) prisons are overcrowded, judges grant probation to repeat offenders and drug dealers. Relatively few crimes are solved and only a small percentage of criminals go to jail.[1]

Tom Kando, Professor of Sociology and Criminal Justice, California State University, Sacramento, says "our criminal justice systems have simply lost the will to combat crime. In fact they implement at every opportunity policies most likely to encourage crime, exclusionary rules and more emphasis on the rights of criminals than those of society.[2]

The Secretary of Health and Human Services now regards violence as a public health issue that affects our entire society, with homicide being a leading cause of death—with a rate that is 4 to 70 times the rate of other countries. It is the leading cause of deaths for Blacks who are 15 to 24 years old and the rate is several times higher than the overall national rate. The Epidemiologic Branch of the Center for Disease Control is now interested in the problem of violence as a public health problem (not just homicide and suicide but child and spouse abuse)—and is extending its research to non-infectious or behavioral causes of illness and death.[3]

We are the most violent society in the western world and have a greater percentage of citizens in jail than any other western country. (The male homicide rate is 12 times Germany's and 5 times Canada's.[4]) For every homicide there are 100 assaults reported to emergency rooms.

People are urged to keep their doors and windows locked, to leave lights on in their homes when they are away and to not open their front doors until the person is identified.

Some authorities suggest that crime in the U.S. is no worse today than in previous periods of history. While it is true that there are cycles in crime rates, I have seen no report in the past 60–70 years that describes anything resembling the situation today. In the words of Vermont Royster, even "The schoolhouse pranks of long ago have yielded to mayhem and even murder in the schools today."

I have been held up at gun point and robbed in broad daylight and our house has been broken into twice. We have never received any feedback from the police who just seem to write up reports for the statistics.

How is this epidemic explained? It seems that it is a reflection of a marked change in society and explanations vary according to individual biases and special interests. Some blame the crime epidemic on the lack of religion—and the decreasing influence it has on people. Others attribute it to drugs and alcohol, to the disintegration of the family, to working mothers and the explosion in the number of latch-key children. Some say it is caused by the violence in movies, and TV, or the influx of large numbers of immigrants and the heterogeneity of the population with its ethnic conflicts; some to the availability of guns, or the population explosion, or the deteriorated educational system and schools, or permissive parents or the opposite—increased child abuse. Some say that children are not needed by their parents as much as before and that they are more often seen as burdens to be raised rather than assets, especially in the increasing number of female headed households and the irresponsibility of the fathers of the legitimate and illegitimate children.

A disproportionate amount of violent crime is committed by gangs in the poorer—lower socio-economic classes and it is the poverty (and unemployment) that is pointed to as the cause—especially when it exists in close proximity to great affluence.

Some blame it on an attitude of entitlement associated with the ever enlarging social programs that stimulate a feeling that someone else is responsible for any deprivation that a person experiences and the anger that arises when expectations of help are not met. Then there are those who attribute the problem to an ineffective criminal justice system with its permissive handling of juvenile offenders—or to a general loss of respect for government the and laws which are not enforced.

Hundreds of millions of dollars have been appropriated by Congress to study crime, find the causes and suggest solutions. Billions have been spent on building prisons. Police forces have been enlarged, and as far as one can tell—all to no avail.

It is helpful to consider how much of crime is a psychiatric problem. (I believe that much of it is.) Children who are persistent deviant lawbreakers are labelled "delinquent" and after they are 18, "antisocial personality disorders." Many of the chronic and violent offenders who are in prisons, have a psychiatric illness. Some are psychotic, some are neurotic, many are substance abusers and have antisocial personalities.

Judge Bazelon, many years ago, regarded the crimes of many of the offenders brought before his court as symptoms of a personality disorder or some other psychiatric diagnosis and believed that such persons should be treated as sick instead of criminals. He saw them as victims of traumatic and/or deprived childhoods.

An increasing number of violent crimes are committed by juveniles who are delinquent but too young to be diagnosed as antisocial personality disorders. These 10 to 17 year old youths, incidentally, are responsible for more than one-half of the serious crime in the U.S.*

It was the recognition of the role that individual psychodynamics and environmental stresses played in the genesis of criminal behavior that in part led to an increased participation of psychiatrists in the criminal justice system. In the state of Washington and perhaps elsewhere, the Departments of Mental Hygiene and Corrections were combined into one. In California the Atascadero State Hospital was used for the incarceration and treatment of sexual psychopaths and the Department of Corrections opened Vacaville, a hospital for the treatment of psychiatrically disordered prisoners (begun in the Terminal Island facility where group therapy and a rehabilitation approach was introduced). In the Youth Authority, procedures were developed to examine juvenile offenders to determine if they needed treatment or confinement. In WWII the Army had established rehabilitation facilities for offenders, who had been given dishonorable discharges and sentenced to prison—where group therapy, designed to help the inmates understand their deviant behavior, was extensively employed.

Increasingly, rehabilitation, rather, than just confinement and punishment, became the goal because some successes were reported using a therapeutic approach. But somehow this didn't bear enough fruit and eventually the conclusion was reached that a therapeutic rehabilitative approach didn't work.[5] Crime got out of hand, many who had been regarded as treatment successes continued their criminal careers after relapse and forensic psychiatrists (of whom there were too few) focused on other problems.

There is no reason not to include the many kinds of persistent law-breaking behavior in adults as psychiatric when such behavior is regarded as in need of psychiatric treatment when it is seen in children and young people. In children it is called "delinquent" or "behavior disorder" and it should be regarded as such in adults.

---

*Thirty years ago, Sen. Daniel Patrick Moynihan of New York warned that the communities where large numbers of young men grew up without fathers have historically been plagued by violence. A study of 57 neighborhoods in 1988 found that the absence of a father was a greater factor than either race or poverty in predicting violent crimes.

In the first part of the century the majority of Black children, like the majority of White children lived in families with mothers and fathers. By the 1980s the number of fatherless families in the Black community increased disproportionately and as a result more young Blacks faced obstacles in their development that contributed to their higher rates of unemployment and crime. (Kamarck, E. C.: Fatherless Families: A Violent Link. *Los Angeles Times,* May 7, 1992; p. B7.)

Social psychiatrists are interested in determining the role that environ-ment, including its culture and characteristics, plays in producing men-tal illnesses and in eliminating those that are identified (in addition to treatment of the individual). When community mental health centers were developed there was some hope they would subserve this function. Unfortunately for the most part—they did not.

So, while the psychopathology of criminal behavior is an appropriate concern for psychiatrists and other mental health professionals, treat-ment of the adult career criminal unfortunately has not been very successful and does not seem to be a promising approach. (This does not preclude treating early young offenders.)

By focusing on the antecedents of crime, however, it may well be possible to make some more effective inroads on the problem. To be sure, the problem of crime is extremely complex and there are undoubtedly multiple causes. One can look at each thing that is blamed and find reason to reject it. All those who are poor don't become criminals. All those who watch all the violence on TV don't become criminals. Nor do those who are unemployed or live in bad neighborhoods.

It is of interest that the dramatic increase in violent crime in the U.S. in the first half of the 1970's (when it seems to have started) was not associated with any increase in poverty or unemployment. In Los Angeles, where, if anything, there was more prosperity and a lower rate of unemployment, homicides increased 31%, violent crimes were up 21% and major crimes 11.4%. Arrests for major crimes were up 12.2%.

During the depression in the 30's with its huge unemployment and poverty, one could walk city streets without fear and there was no need for armed guards in schoolhouse halls. As has been pointed out by others it isn't as if the current wave of violent crime was due to hunger or involved a loaf of bread. Muggings and robberies are not because chil-dren are starving. Food stamps and welfare have taken care of that and it isn't as if violent crimes were being selectively committed by the poor against the rich. The poor, along with the aged and infirm, are the ones who are more likely than others to be the victims. *Time Magazine* has observed that the poor are most inclined to steal from other poor in their own neighborhoods, and, according to victims, police and social workers, younger and younger youths (boys and girls) are involved in more widespread senseless violence than at any time in the recent past. They come primarily from a segment of society that is poor and regarded as "the left-behind minorities who see no stake in preserving the way things are and who see crime as the only way to get one's fair share in an unfair world."

According to Phil Kirby, violent street crime "is the symptom of an ominous social disorder—the development in this country of a permanent underclass, conditioned by its circumstances to violence, and deeply alienated from traditional values." He points out that it is not the children of Beverly Hills who are carrying guns and that almost all of the juveniles in a California Youth Authority prison were uneducated, barely literate and never held a job long, if at all. He predicted that they will "graduate" into the adult correctional system by committing new crimes.[6]

Many studies have confirmed the higher incidence of crime in lower social classes and minorities when poverty is associated with excessive family stress, child abuse and neglect, poor health and negative attitudes toward life.

So, it is in the early family experiences that we must look to explain the crime epidemic. And these are in turn associated with some dramatic changes in society that are contributing. If crime is to be prevented—it is on these two causes that attention must be directed.

The fact that children reared in poverty are more apt to be exposed to crime, drugs, prostitution, robbery and fencing, doesn't explain why some get involved in these activities while others do not. It is only reasonable to ask: "Where are his/her parents when the young potential criminal is learning from the fences, the pushers and older boys, and getting money for movies, candy, baseballs, radios, and jewelry. Where do they think he is getting the money and how much do they care?"

There is abundant clinical evidence of the importance of intact families, of having two parents who are concerned and loving, who set standards and good examples and have positive expectations for their children, in producing law-abiding children. Where there is no caring person in the family who presents clear standards and high expectations and there is serious marital discord or disruption, abuse, alcoholism, lack of financial support, there is a greater likelihood of the children becoming delinquent and it is the delinquent juvenile who more often becomes the adult criminal.

A comparison of the background of adolescent female inmates of the Illinois State Training School for girls showed that those who needed special treatment because of their continued non-conforming behavior had, more serious psychiatric diagnoses, a higher rate of illegitimate births, greater family disorganization (with less time with father and mother), parents who were more abnormal with more overt psychopathology, and delinquency that started at an earlier age. When compared with inmates who were conformers, they were four times as likely to belong to a minority racial-ethnic group and three times as likely to come from a slum or ghetto. They were less educated, had lower I.Q.'s and three times the normal rate of living in a broken nuclear family.

There have been the innumerable studies that have clearly shown how early life plays a crucial role and that Black children have a special problem. Repeated studies have shown that Black offenders account not for a majority but for a disproportionate number of robberies, murder, rape and aggravated assault. Some have tried to attribute this to their greater poverty but as Silberman has pointed out, Puerto Ricans in New York City are poorer than Blacks, have less education and more often hold menial jobs, and although the groups are roughly comparable in size, Blacks are much more often (63.5% vs 15.3%) arrested for violent crimes. Similar and equally striking differences are experienced in San Antonio where the predominant population is Spanish American, and in Arizona.[7]

The high violent crime rate in Black youths has developed during a time when great advances were made in civil rights and educational and economic opportunities. It also developed during a period of greater disruption in Black family life and of a greater reliance on welfare. It is likely that playing significant roles are the absence of proper family and parental influence that has assisted other minority groups to emerge from poverty. The welfare system that was developed out of humane and altruistic motives has had an unfortunate result of fostering a degree of dependency (along with an attitude of entitlement) that is said to have destroyed the fabric of the Black ghetto society. More than one half of all Black children are now brought up outside the nuclear family as opposed to under 20% of Whites. "This tragedy of family breakdown which doubled in dimensions during the decade after 1964 is chiefly the product of guilt ridden blandishments and subsidies of White liberalism."[8]

William Raspberry, points out how Black leaders attribute the staggering unemployment rate among Black youths to "The System." They say the racist system doesn't promote education of Black children and racist employers don't provide the job opportunities for the Black teenagers. These same Black leaders however "do not waste time railing against the system when it comes to their own children." Instead, they work at getting their children ready to take advantage of the opportunities that exist. They tell their children to modify their language, dress and behavior to create favorable impressions. They tell their children, "They will be confronted with racism" but that doesn't mean that they should give up, only that they must try twice as hard, be twice as good. While they are quite willing to say these things privately to their own children, they are afraid to say them publicly to other people's children—lest White people hear them and assume they no longer need to feel guilty. What they say in public to "keep the pressure on the system" is heard by other people's children—who may come to see themselves as hopeless victims of a racist system they are powerless to change. He believes it would be helpful for these youngsters to be taught the importance of doing what they can for themselves instead of waiting for others to change the system.[9]

What isn't recognized is that there are many parents who (for whatever reason) are incapable of rearing mentally healthy, law abiding children and that alternatives must be provided. Many have mentioned the extremely high death rate from murder seen in young Black males. It is twenty times the comparable White rate and, for the most part, it is Blacks killing, raping and robbing Blacks. In fact, Blacks are probably more afraid of Black violence than are Whites—and they are no longer inclined to emphasize poverty and racism as the cause (as they did previously)—nor a selective bias of the police.

Studies have clearly shown that parent's behavior patterns are good predictors of their children's adult behavior. Sociopathic men pass their behavior patterns on to their children. Most antisocial children who are involved in theft, truancy, incorrigibility, etc., had deviant family backgrounds, came from disrupted and often impoverished homes and have fathers who are sociopathic and/or alcoholic. They usually live in lower-class neighborhoods where there are other children who are truant, stealing and undisciplined. As adults they have a high rate of arrests and imprisonment, poor occupational and personal adjustment, extensive use of welfare services and excessive use of alcohol and other drugs. Severe behavior disorders, starting with hyperactivity and uncontrollability, occurred in 3/4 of the children abused by their families and usually progressed to adult criminality.[10]

At a recent meeting of the American Association for the Advancement of Science, it was pointed out how children who were abused or neglected were more likely than others to be arrested as juveniles and as adults—(and to be alcohol and drug abusers, unemployed and mentally disordered).

What chance does a child have to become a law abiding citizen who grows up in a crowded city neighborhood where there is a mixture of cultures, where distrust and hostility prevail, where housing is poor, where there are many unemployed and many on welfare, or involved in prostitution, drug use or pushing: where the child is exposed to juvenile delinquents, hard core criminals, pimps and deinstitutionalized psychotics—where the population feels victimized, alienated, segregated and hostile toward the police? What chance does the child have who is reared in such an environment by a teenage mother who is a school dropout, without a husband and whose own mother was never married, was on welfare and never had any work experience, or whose father was an alcoholic who abused his wife and children and exposed them to perpetual neglect?

Ashley Montague, quite sometime ago, pointed out how many people were totally unprepared for and incapable of being parents. He said, "Man is the only 150 lb non-linear servomechanism that can be wholly reproduced by unskilled labor." Nevertheless they are permitted to bring innumerable children into the world, the responsibility for whom falls on a society that not only doesn't assume it, but protects and defends the right of these people to go on proliferating when at the same time it insists on people passing tests to drive a car, install a toilet or build a house. Statistics show this is no small problem. From 1960 to 1986 the percent of adolescent mothers (17 or younger) who were not married when they gave birth increased from 15% to more than 60%.[11]

Parents claim they can't control their children and society doesn't want to take over the job. Unfortunately, the foster home program for children who are removed from incapable and abusive parents, has not been the answer.

No longer does there seem to be any question that childhood environment is critical. It can contribute to antisocial behavior and is the greatest predictor of future adjustment to life.

It should be possible to identify a child needing help through school records—since truancy and poor school performance are nearly universally present in pre-sociopaths. If the home situation cannot be straightened out, the child should be removed from the home, if adult sociopathic behavior is to be prevented.

Kenneth Schoen, formerly the Corrections Commissioner of the State of Minnesota, maintains that "the real answer to America's intolerable crime and crack problem is to be found by noticing who is in our prisons—inmates drawn almost exclusively from the ranks of the poor, Blacks, and Latinos. Doing something about the conditions that generate this lopsided situation is complicated, but at the most basic level it means changing the environments in which the young see graffiti before they see any beauty, hear gun shots before symphonies and feel despair before hope. That's a tough order, but we can start by being honest about what does not work."[12]

We should not ignore a survey of Baltimore public school students that showed that 59% of the males who came from one-parent or no-parent homes carried a handgun. In four years the number of young Black males who were killed by guns more than doubled (and the rate was 11 times higher than in Whites).[13] "Predators in our Society aren't born, they are made"—"they as we, are shaped by their environment."[14]

California State Senator David Roberti called attention to studies, showing that children who witness or are abused by domestic violence have the tendency to express this when they are adults. Eighty to 90% of prison inmates give histories of having been abused or of having witnessed domestic violence when they were children. At San Quentin, 100% of the inmates were abused when young.[15]

In addition to identifying the children who are the potential criminals and of providing a proper environment for them, some changes in society will be needed if crime is to be controlled. In the past 40 years there has been a much needed emphasis on individual rights—but unfortunately it was accompanied by a disregard of the rights of society. Aid to families with dependent children, rent subsidies, food stamps, job training, affirmative action, equal employment opportunity, loans to minority businesses, head start, scholarships, child care centers and family planning—all of which were intended to assist the poor, reduce stress and improve the quality of life—have unfortunately had no effect on the incidence of crime or for that matter on mental health.

As Thomas Sowell (who had a great influence on Judge Clarence Thomas), in his book on race and economics, points out, subsidies and preferential treatment are being employed to improve ethnic minority income instead of promoting those methods that have historically proven successful—self-reliance, work skills, education and experience—all of which are slow developing. What should be provided are jobs.[16]

People seem to be more anxious, more depressed, more hostile, more dependent and less able to get along with each other, if one is to judge by the disintegration of families, the increased number of divorces, the increase in violence and substance abuse. Questions are being raised about the possible relationship between pop lyrics and violent crimes against women.[17] A recent album is laced with graphic lyrics about beating, raping and murdering women. The message given is that violence against women is fun and defended as "free speech." The suicide rate of adolescents has reached unprecedented heights and there has been a progressive decrease in the quality of life despite more widespread ownership of cars, televisions, stereos, jewelry and money for other nonnecessities.

Loitering and vagrancy, which used to be crimes, are now accepted and defended as rights and most communities are confronted with increasing numbers of homeless living on their streets and in their parks.

Violence in language has been commented on by the late Norman Cousins who said bad speech was becoming almost as casual as the possession of handguns, bad dress, bad manners and bad human relationships.[18]

Less than 10% of American households now consist of a full-time, stay-at-home mother, a father who is working and minor children—and we have the highest teenage pregnancy and abortion rates in the western world.

Most persons seem to be more willing to accept all of the crime and violence and, the deterioration in the quality of life associated with it, than to accept any infringement on their freedom. Any restriction of their mobility—to go anywhere they wish without being questioned—is equated with totalitarian, fascist, nazi, or communist states. They would rather have the crime. It's as if there were no in-between. Americans reject the idea of a national identification card as an infringement of their freedom and anonymity. It is this irrational fear of having to give up some of their rights that accounts in part for the lack of public outrage and demonstrations against having to live in a jungle. People will march in protest and demonstrate against the absence of a traffic light, or a nuclear electrical generating plant, the use of animals in medical research, or the threatened deportation of a homosexual—but not against the muggings and killing they are victims of in broad daylight and in their own homes.

William Grieder has described "The Moral Liberation of American Society" by the following changes that have taken place: Long standing religious commandments and social taboos have fallen; Protestant disapproval of gambling was displaced by multimillion dollar public lotteries, sponsored by state and local governments; Pornography, once forbidden and furtive became freely available; Homosexuality and prostitution were reconsidered in a more tolerant light; Morale inhibitors that had held authority for centuries were abandoned; Old notions of sinfulness were redefined as largely private matters.

It would appear that the defective upbringing of the juvenile criminal does not provide the example or incentive to sublimate the aggressive primitive drives that may persist in man. The California Commission on Crime Control and Violence in its report of 1/15/82 agreed with the U.S. Attorney General's Task Force on Violent Crime's conclusion that it was a breakdown of the social order, not the legal order, that was reflected in the wave of violent crime, and that "only we as a society, as parents, as caring human beings, can prevent our children from becoming violent adults."

Howard Smith, the black ex-addict who worked in the U.S. Government Manpower Project to assist the hard core welfare recipients (some of whom were ex-criminals) to become self-sufficient, provides a graphic description of the change that has taken place in society. He says, "The difference between his generation and the majority of hard core group he worked with is that even though we may have had a female-oriented family, the average mother in the 1940's and 50's had different values— welfare was wrong, drugs were wrong. Every Sunday you had to put on a blue serge suit and a pair of shoes and go to church. You may not have been getting the best education in a segregated school, but you had to go to school. And they thought nothing about cutting your behind with a strap. You respected your elders and didn't talk back. Those mothers were tough. Today it's a new ball game. The kids aren't taught these same values. Now it's the parents whose behinds get cut with a strap. You have parents who are actually afraid of their kids." He adds, "I'm frightened when I see a bunch of young kids on the street late at night. We have a generation of people coming up now with no family structure and, those who want government to do more do not want to look at the family disruption, out-of-wedlock births, teenage pregnancies, and the lack of a healthy childhood environment, lest it decrease government effort and demand more of the individual."[20]

Most believe that programs that were designed to benefit minorities (costing over one trillion dollars over the past 25 years) have not worked and ask "Why do so many Blacks, after three decades of civil rights and vast national support, drop out of school, choose destructive lifestyles and end up on welfare or in jail."

Although the vast majority of Blacks in America are decent, law abiding, hard working people, Whites are increasingly unwilling to shoulder the blame for the majority of Black children who are born to unwed mothers and the disintegration of the Black family.

Many Whites feel threatened by the violence and crime committed by lawless young Blacks who provide some reality basis for the irrational identification of Blacks with crime that is promoted by many TV movies. Whites increasingly see not Blacks but themselves as victims of crime and violence and see their fear as justified. They no longer support the idea of special preference in hiring, promotion, and college admission. Such preferences are now regarded as reverse racism. The undisguised hatred for Whites by Blacks in the recent Los Angeles riots is indicative of Black racism that is rarely if ever mentioned.[21] Black policemen are criticized by Black racists who insist that color should determine one's behavior and thinking. They ask, "Are you Black or are you blue?"

A change in philosophy of the school system is described by Daniel Boorstin who has written about the "decline of grammar and the colloquial conquering of the classroom."

He relates how Charles Carpenter, a Professor of Linguistics, banished such terms as "mistake," "correct" and "error" from his vocabulary and urged all English teachers to do the same. Use of the word "whom" was too high class and it was okay for a boy to say, "I didn't see no dog," since what he was saying was clear (even if incorrect)."

Art too changed and people became less certain whether what they were seeing was really art. There were changes in standards of behavior along with changes in attitude toward nudity and morals. Science replaced religion and instead of "Thou shall not" there was speculation about the nature of man. Psychologists, Boorstin said, "strove to liberate men from taboos and inhibitions of an authoritarian Protestant morality" contributing, thereby, to the sexual revolution (which needs no description) and in all probability to crime. Understanding misbehavior seemed more important than stopping it or punishing it.[22]

Lance Morrow described the deterioration in social habit in the U.S. "Since the end of World War II, Americans have been steadily relinquishing their inhibitions about the social consequences of their actions. They have lost a crucial sense of community, while highways, jets, satellite TV signals and leisure travel have brought them physically closer together. The social environment has grown polluted with a head-long greed and self-absorption. Somehow, Americans have also misplaced the moral confidence with which to condemn sleaziness and stupidity. It is as if something in the American judgment snapped and has remained so long unrepaired that no one notices anymore." He says, "Americans have too much freedom, without discipline, without a sense of being responsible and useful in the world. Their angers spill and slop like battery acids."[23]

Marvin Stone attributed our astounding crime rate "to a lack of ethics, which in turn is due to a lack of ethical instruction in schools and other opinion-forming institutions."[24]

It is not generally known that Dwight Eisenhower was concerned about the future of the country. He wondered if there were some validity to the communist belief that man was incapable of self-government because of his intimate selfishness and the conflicts among pressure groups. The difficulties encountered in democratic systems is the conse-quence of an inability of men to forego immediate gain for a long-time good. He believed we do not have a sufficient number of people who are ready to make the immediate sacrifice in the form of a long-term investment. It has been said that "we get the criminals our society deserves" and that "what degree of domestic tranquility and freedom from crime that we have is mostly because individuals choose to conform to the law and not because of the police and court activities."[25]

There are conflicting opinions about gun control and the degree to which the availability of guns contribute to the epidemic of violent crime. In one Southern city, a police sergeant not only defends the right of a citizen to carry a gun, but sees the need for citizens to protect themselves since the police have not been able to stop the increase in violent crimes. Furthermore, it is claimed that there is no truly conclu-sive evidence that the ready availability of guns increase the amount of crime.

Experts differ on whether people should try to defend themselves against violent criminals. There are those who advocate karate or judo lessons, instruction in the use of mace, gauging eyes or traumatizing testicles. There are others in much greater numbers who advise complete compliance with the request of the attacking criminal with no effort at self-protection or calling for help and even carrying money at all times to keep a hold-up man from getting frustrated or angry. People no longer believe the police can protect them and are told so by the police.

Violent crime is reported as having spread to the suburbs and rural areas out of the cities where it was traditionally located—and the crimes are becoming more brutal, more irrational and more random. The criminals, and especially the young ones, more and more resemble wild animals, and the victimized public (according to a Houston Police Chief) is living more like animals behind protective bars, locks and alarms. A justice department study found that one out of every three households in the United States was directly affected by some kind of serious crime in the preceding year.

Violent crimes are committed by gangs against other groups—sometimes making mistakes and killing innocent bystanders. Many are committed by people who are associated in one way or another with the victims, but an increasing number, now estimated to be one-third, are by someone the victim never met, sometimes in the course of a robbery but sometimes without any identifiable reason. It is the latter type that arouses the most fear. A former director of the Bureau of Justice Statistics predicted that within a few years every household in the country will be hit by crime.

Crime rates in Los Angeles, New York, Miami and other cities have been increasing. According to the police, there is a breed of mean, antisocial, impulse ridden young people, many on drugs, who have no respect for the law or society's mores, who are proud and brag to their associates about their senseless, random, vicious murder and assaults.

There are many who believe that most of the muggings and robberies are done by drug addicts who are desperate for a "fix" and will do anything to obtain the money for it. Because there is an intimate relationship between crime and substance abuse, various programs to reduce crime have involved treatment of the substance abuser. Substituting supervised methadone maintenance administration for drug abuse, has permitted some addicts to become socially productive and to avoid criminal behavior in which they had previously been engaged. Alcoholics Anonymous and other diversion programs and antabuse have helped many alcoholics to remain sober and free of antisocial and violent behavior.

Naltrexone has been used as an alternative to confinement. Inmates with a history of opiate addiction have traditionally been excluded from jail work release programs because of the great likelihood they would return to drug use. A Nassau County (N.Y.) program was adopted for inmates who agreed to taking the medication twice weekly and have routine checks for drugs and alcohol. Because Naltrexone (as compared to Methadone) has no street value it does not engender criminal activity. An uncashed paycheck must be turned in each week as proof of having worked all week. Part of the money is applied toward the cost of room and board and 10% placed in a trust account. While each program has some success, there has been no appreciable reduction in crime or drug abuse and the need for additional prisons continues at an unabated rate.

Homes of working couples make tempting targets for daytime burglaries by unattended sons of working couples, and a large share of all violent crime is committed by a surprisingly small group of hard-core criminals. In Washington, D.C., seven percent of criminals arrested in a 4½ year period had been arrested four times. This seven percent accounted for 24 percent of all the serious crimes that were solved in those years.

The criminal justice system too gets blamed for much of the crime problem. A majority of criminals are never arrested and even when arrested, a majority go unpunished. For example, in New York State of 130,000 felony arrests a year, 8,000 go to prison. In New York City, of 94,000 felony arrests. 5 to 6,000 serve time. In the District of Columbia it was 116 out of 6,000 incidents of aggravated assault.

The courts blame the police and the police blame the courts. There are long delays in bringing criminals to trial. Witnesses disappear, victims get over being acutely upset and trials deteriorate to consideration of legal technicalities instead of what the public regards as the truth or justice.

Marvin Wolfgang of the University of Pennsylvania followed 10,000 males born in Philadelphia in 1948—627 had five arrests by the time they were adults but they accounted for two-thirds of all the violent crimes attributed to the group and almost all the homicides. James Q. Wilson points out that juvenile records are confidential and at 18 a young man's record is considered clean no matter how many crimes he had committed before that. Punishment for crime has neither been certain, prompt nor appropriate partly because shrewd lawyers employ technicalities to keep felons from going to prison in the first place.

Gun Control laws, it is said, will not prevent the kinds of murders that are committed by criminals in cities that already have tough gun control laws. The country knows something is wrong. Too many people are angry, too many losing hope, hooked on drugs or emotionally disturbed. Too many are turning to crimes of violence. The notion that this can be changed by controlling guns . . . may be an excuse for avoiding the hard work of making our decrepid criminal justice system start to function and the even harder work of buttressing what used to be called the nation's "moral fiber." Washington, D.C., with one of the toughest anti-gun laws, is said to have the highest murder rate in the country.[26]

A change in the criminal justice system is needed. As one writer asked, why, in a country where there are no Kangaroo courts, no arbitrary imprisonment, no prison without a public trial and no political kidnappings or disappearances is there such concern about the rights of criminals and disregard of the rights of society—for which the criminal laws were also written?

The chances of a crime leading to an arrest, conviction and serious prison term are well under one in one hundred in many parts of the country. Although we have more people in jail than ever before, a rational criminal can calculate the odds that crime does pay. Gun control proposals only hide the deeper problem that the country still lacks the will to punish criminals.[27]

Chief Justice Burger claimed "The massive safeguards for accused persons, built up by the judicial system in recent decades are out of proportion with the protection afforded to law abiding citizens." He called for swift arrest, prompt trials and finality of judgment to deter crime.[28]

The protection of juvenile criminals because they are young is in part responsible for the great increase in crime. It is claimed that juvenile courts and detention centers have become havens of refuge and privileged sanctuaries for youthful offenders guilty of first-degree murder and violent, serious crime.

"Robert, one of three boys who raped and sodomized an elderly bag lady in New York's Central Park and was the one who beat her to death with a stick afterward, was given the maximum penalty of 18 months provided by New York law for any act, even murder, committed by a person 12 years of age or younger." Another boy with six previous appearances in Family Court on robbery charges who, on being arrested for purse grabbing and knocking victims to the ground, said, "go on, call the cops, they can't do nothing to me. I ain't 16 yet."

Generally the juvenile criminal who commits a brutal act of random violence must receive the least restrictive punishment. He enjoys anonymity in the courtroom that is closed to the press and the public in order to avoid being stigmatized, and legal technicalities are often used to prevent any punishment. There are many persons who encourage

young repeated offenders to believe that society is picking on them
unfairly and that society is to blame for their problem. They didn't go to
school, didn't want to look for a job or take one that wasn't good enough.
Sociologists and psychologists are inclined to blame anything but the
individual himself.[29]

Senator Edward Kennedy warned that crime reform depended on
making the justice system fairer. He would eliminate juvenile courts for
violent youths as an unrealistic attempt at humaneness that has backfired.

A New York survey found out that of nearly 4,000 juveniles arrested
for robbery in one year, only 118 received some custodial sentence. In
1974 there were 4,847 juveniles arrested in New York City for 5,666
violent crimes—9% were convicted and only 40% of these (or 3.6%)
were incarcerated in a training school, prison or other institution.
Legal restraints prevent police from fingerprinting or photographing
juveniles and deny judges access to the sealed records of convicted
criminals.

The 300% increase in the nation's crime occurred precisely in the
years when society was at its greatest pains to humanize the justice
system, make rehabilitation programs work and relax the law's suppos-
edly heartless rigidity (by allowing indeterminate sentences). Barbara
Boland of the Washington Urban Institute pointed out that most crime is
now committed by a large number of mostly young offenders—too young
and too numerous to be clearly identified as habitual offenders. They
constitute 15% of the urban male population between ages 14 and 29 and
account for 85% of all serious crime.

Chronic offenders (those who were arrested at least six times) commit
20 to 30 serious crimes from age 14 to 29. Since in only 5 to 10% is there a
conviction, they typically are convicted only two or three times. So, in
the District of Columbia, the overwhelming majority of crimes go
unpunished.

A Rand Corporation study found that between the ages of 16 and 22
each of a group of more serious offenders committed between 18 and 40
crimes a year and concluded that the greatest effect in crime prevention
would come from imprisoning the younger more active offenders. A
meager arrest record often disguised a very active and dangerous
criminal.[30]

Walter Miller of the Harvard Law School Center for Criminal Justice
found that the bulk of serious, violent and predatory crime in the U.S. is

committed by youths under 21. Wilson and others claim that incarcerating young recidivists for a year would result in a 50% reduction in the crime rate. It seems clear that drastic changes are needed.

It seems to me that many people who are confined to prison for non-violent crimes can be required to make restitution and pay the penalty for the crimes by community service and fines without having to be locked up. They could continue to be productive and remain an asset instead of a liability to society. There are violent criminals who must be removed from society. There are pros and cons for the death penalty. Life imprisonment is an alternative that is not only very costly to society, but inhumane. There must be a better way than putting someone for the duration of his life, in a cage like an animal, one that would not necessitate the huge expense of building top security cells and the approximate $30,000 a year that it costs to maintain the criminal in it. A Devil's Island type of facility would make much better sense. There are islands off the coast that could be utilized and accomplish what is needed in a more humane way. Criminals would engage in raising much of their own food and have some responsibility for the operation and governance of their own society. The problem of possible escape would require solution. With all of our technological advances it should certainly be possible.

A preventive approach is needed if the crime problem is to be controlled. It will involve the early identification of the potential criminal—when behavioral and antisocial manifestations are seen in elementary school and the institution of corrective action—that may involve correcting a disturbed or pathological home situation, and providing school programs, day centers and residential facilities for the child who is in a malignant environment. The American Psychiatric Association Handbook on Psychiatric Practice in Juvenile Court (in press) says "One of the most critical problems is the lack of adequate residential and community programs for troubled youths. The most difficult issue is the terminating of parenthood rights. Psychiatry has failed to effect many deviant parenting practices.

Also needed is a change in the philosophy of the school system and greater emphasis on the rights of society than has been the case in the past 40 or 50 years. There will have to be more emphasis on proper behavior and less on just doing your own thing. There are such things as morality and consideration for others. We need to recover from the "Poverty of Spirit" a term used by Martin Luther King. Finally—a drastic change in the criminal justice system is required.

David Gurgen suggested that instead of being briefed by the CIA and National Security Advisors, the President be told that in the past 24 hours 93 Americans died from guns, 16,000 were raped, mugged and robbed, 274 babies were born exposed to illicit drugs, 2,478 children quit school and 1,240 teenagers gave birth. What is needed is a change of mind about what is urgent.[31]

The young secretary who gave much generous help with her typing of this report pointed out that I had failed to discuss and recommend a solution to the problem that she and many mothers like her face. She has a small daughter who is just entering kindergarten. There is only her mother (who is not in the best of health) to look after the child when school lets out. She earns too much money to qualify for subsidized child care and not enough to pay the full price of a private child care facility. Therefore, she has no choice but to depend on her mother. She is a mother who is interested in bringing up her child in a safe and nurturing environment — but is afraid of the consequences she will have to face if her mother (for one reason or another) is no longer able to care for her child.

She seemed to resent the fact that the rich and very poor can obtain assistance very readily, while many others like herself cannot. This points to the desperate need for child care facilities for the increasing number of working mothers who are trying to support themselves and their children. If a child has no place to go, he may just end up in the streets, committing crimes.

Crime is intimately related to drug abuse, and prevention of one will also contribute to the prevention of the other. Both are in turn related to poverty. What is needed is a societal change that will deal with the practices and characteristics of our society that have been identified as the causes of the agony these problems are now creating.

REFERENCES

1. *Wall Street Journal,* March 19, 1991; p. A-24.
2. *Wall Street Journal,* March 19, 1991; p. A-24.
3. Check, W.A.; Public Health Problems of Violence Receive Epidemiologic Attention. *JAMA,* August 16, 1985; 254:881–92.
4. *Wall Street Journal,* June 24, 1991; p. A-10.
5. McDonald, M.: *Psychiat. News,* February 6, 1976; XI:3 p. 1.
6. *L. A. Times,* December 4, 1980; Part II. p. 1.
7. *Criminal Violence, Criminal Justice.* Random House, 1978; p. 118.
8. Gilder, G.: The Aftermath of Slavery's Last Days. *Wall Street Journal,* July 13, 1979.

9. Joblessness: Isn't It the Only Culprit. *L. A. Times,* December 29, 1980.

10. Oliver & Buchanon: *British Journal of Psychiat.,* 1979. 135:289.

11. *Annals of Internal Medicine,* April 1, 1991. 114:559.

12. *L. A. Times,* August 15, 1989; Part II. p. 7.

13. Watkin, G.: *U.S. News and World Report,* April 5, 1991; p. 26.

14. Kerby, P.: *L. A. Times,* July 23, 1981; Part III. p. 1.

15. *L. A. Reporter,* October 14, 1981; p. 2.

16. *The Economics and Politics of Race.* Morrow, New York, 1983.

17. Phillips, C.: *L. A. Times,* July 23, 1991; p. F-3.

18. *Time,* April 2, 1990; p. 18.

19. *Secrets of the Temple.* Simon & Schuster, New York, 1987; p. 170.

20. Auletta, K.: *The Underclass.* Random House, New York, 1982.

21. Zuckerman, M.B.: Editorial, Black and White American. *U.S. News & World Report,* October 28, 1991; p. 92.

22. *The Americans, the Democratic Experience.* Vintage Books, New York, 1974; p. 451.

23. *Time,* February 4, 1980; p. 86.

24. *U.S. News and World Report,* January 22, 1979; p. 80.

25. *L. A. Times,* April 1, 1979; Part V. p. 3.

26. *Wall Street Journal,* Editorial, December 19, 1981.

27. *Wall Street Journal,* April 5, 1991; p. A-14.

28. *Time,* February 23, 1981; p. 81.

29. Kramer, R.: One the Case of Young Thugs. *Wall Street Journal,* June 3, 1986; p. 30.

30. *Mental Health Scope.* September 19, 1977; Vol XI, No. 16, p. 7.

31. *U.S. News and World Report,* June 17, 1991; p. 68.

Chapter 3

POVERTY*

Poverty in the United States is defined annually by the minimum income a non-farm family of four needs for a subsistence diet, housing, clothing, medical expense and other essentials and is calculated by multiplying the cost of food by three. It is geared to providing comfort rather than mere survival. It has been said that the poor in the United States are the best housed, fed and clothed in the world. Those who are suffering from chronic poverty, who are not elderly, blind or totally disabled, are primarily those families with dependent children, judging from the number on welfare.

According to government figures poverty among the aged dropped from 55% in 1959 to 14.1% in 1983 as a result of the Social Security program. Since 1983 there has been a further decrease in the number of aged poor as payments were linked to increases in the cost of living. Poverty among children, however, has climbed and now includes approximately one fourth of all children in the United States.[1]

A family with a woman at the head is many times more likely to be poor than a family headed by a man or a married couple and more than half of the children who live in female-headed households in the United States are growing up in poverty.[2] There is some evidence that the increase in single mothers is caused by changed attitudes toward family life and sexual conduct than by the availability of welfare.

Black children and those born to unwed mothers are the most likely to be poor. Almost half of all Black children and more than one third of all Hispanic children are poor (in contrast to approximately 16% of all White children. A congressional study (in 1983) revealed that almost 20% of births in 1983 were to unwed mothers and 75% of such children were poor.[3]

An increase in divorces and out of wedlock births with the corresponding

---

*Parts of this chapter are from "Poverty and Mental Illness," *American Journal of Psychiatry,* 1969; 125:1172.

increase in female headed families added greatly to the number of poor. Everyone whose sole income is Aid to Families with Dependent Children (AFDC) can be safely said to be poor.[2]

According to a 1974 government report, 34% of all families headed by a woman were living in poverty, with the percentage of such Black, Mexican American and Puerto Rican families being at least twice that of White women. The greater the number of children, the greater was the percentage in poverty. Approximately 75% to 81% of those with six or more children were poor in contrast to 11% to 22% when there were no children under 18.[4]

The poor are an extremely heterogenous group that includes the aged poor who were not poor earlier in life and those who were. There are also the working poor, the disabled who are unable to work, those unable to get jobs, and some of the mentally ill, alcoholics, addicted, homeless, students, drop-outs and criminals.

Poverty may be acute, chronic or intermittent. It varies in severity. Rural poverty is different from urban poverty. Poor is not synonymous with lower social class or blue collar class. Many blue collar industrial workers who are not poor are regarded as class IV or V (the two lowest socio-economic classes on a scale of 1 to 5.), and many elderly who have become destitute are not in the lower social classes.

In the past few years, the number of persons sliding into poverty has exceeded the number who have emerged. As of 1991, 13% or over 30 million persons in the U.S. were classified as poor, and there is no question that greater attention is now being paid to the problem of poverty.[5] No longer are the poor in this country regarded in accordance with religious doctrine as courageous, noble, kind and Godlike. They constitute a social problem that many feel can be solved by spending enough money or bringing about a more equitable distribution of wealth.[6]

Many of the chronic poor of America today are a residual group with a disproportionate number of Blacks, Mexican Americans and Puerto Ricans who have not been able to take part in the general social mobility to get themselves above the poverty level. Some believe this is because of something inherent in this residual group that is not present in others like them who do succeed and was not present in the large number of immigrants who came to the U.S. In the past, the poor and destitute worked in the least desirable jobs, and lived in crowded cheap tenements but who through their own motivation and effort made their way out of lives of poverty. Others attribute it to the fact that the culture and circumstances have changed so much in recent years that the achievements of the immigrants of the past are no longer possible.[7]

WHY POVERTY?

The Bible says 'ye have the poor always with you' and there has never been a time in history, nor a nation that did not have its poor. In the past it was assumed that there would always be the poor and that somehow the poor were to be rewarded in Heaven—so they shouldn't mind being poor on Earth. Now with a secular approach, there is the expectation that all problems of man and society can be solved. Hence the search for the causes of poverty.

A change in the American culture has occurred with the recent emphasis on rights rather than obligations (what has been called the galloping psychology of entitlement), on egalitarianism (despite obvious differences in competence, skill, knowledge, intelligence, motivation, etc.) and on evolving a welfare state (rather than a society in which a person is expected to be responsible for himself). There seems to be an increasing expectation that one should have to do only that work that one enjoys and work is no longer regarded as something that must be done in order to survive.

We have become the world's most litigious society with an attitude that if something bad or untoward happens to a person it is someone else's fault. Poverty is now regarded as one such misfortune for which society now accepts primary responsibility—thereby diminishing individual motivation to find solutions or remedies.

Some give psychological explanations for the persistent residual group of poor, pointing to personality characteristics that preclude a solution. Some find sociological reasons—like racial prejudice and lack of equal opportunities in education and work, and discrimination against females and some minority groups. Others provide geographical explanations like the existence of areas in the deep South and Appalachia where poverty is the normal state. The feeling is that someone who is unfortunate to be born or living in a poverty area is likely to be condemned to poverty unless he moves elsewhere. Some blame society for poverty and accuse the non-poor of exploiting the poor for their own advantage and purposefully perpetuating the poor.

The unprecedented industrial development with its mechanization, automation, and mass production that has occurred in this century is believed to be partly responsible for the problem of chronic poverty. A change has been particularly pronounced in American agriculture where large-scale commercial enterprises have replaced many small farms. There have been marked increases in farm production, while the number of those employed in production has declined both relatively and absolutely. In the United States, certain minorities (Blacks, Mexican Americans, American Indians and Puerto Ricans) have traditionally been engaged in non-mechanized farm work and they are the ones who are most apt to be victims of the change, and many of those who do find full employment at such work are still materially deprived.

The Southern (rural) to Northern (urban) migration of twentieth-century American Blacks can thus be seen as agricultural displacement. Unfortunately, much of this migration has taken place at a time when the need for unskilled labor in the industrial cities of the North has decreased, leaving little aside from marginal occupations. Furthermore, discrimination and racist attitudes have further attenuated the opportunity structure as they affect employer policy as well as union recruitment.[8]

Machines now do a lot of the heavy work that was previously done by men and jobs that were time consuming are now done much more quickly. Heavy, backbreaking labor of the kind that used to be regularly associated with bull gangs or concrete gangs is no longer characteristic of laboring jobs, especially those with the larger, well-equipped construction companies. Brute strength is still required from time to time, as on smaller jobs where it is not economical to bring in heavy equipment or where the small, undercapitalized contractor has none to bring in. In many cases, however, the conveyor belt has replaced the wheelbarrow or the Georgia buggy; mechanized forklifts have eliminated heavy, manual lifting; and a variety of digging machines have replaced the pick and shovel. The result is fewer jobs for unskilled laborers and, in many cases, a work speed-up for those who do have jobs.[9]

As a result poorly educated, unskilled persons who are disproportionately represented in the chronic poor have greater difficulty finding jobs. This may be a factor in their abandoning one way or another wives and children who then constitute the major fraction of the chronic poor.

It is interesting, however, that some of the unemployed poor who receive assistance will not take jobs that they regard as menial. It is difficult for many to understand why with so much unemployment and so many receiving one or another kind of governmental assistance, large numbers of illegal aliens must be brought into the United States for farm and other labor.

Christopher Jencks, a sociologist at Northwestern University in his book, *Rethinking Social Policy* (Harvard University Press), concluded that many young Blacks refuse to take minimum wage jobs because they regard them as subservient ones that are offered by Whites.

PERSONALITY FACTORS IN POVERTY

In our market or money economy every person is supposed to learn the standard acquisitive skills, usually in the family, in childhood. In middle class families there is an emphasis on this and stability, and there are examples for children to learn from and to imitate. The same patterns of socialization (including skills of acquisitiveness) do not always exist in poor families. One study of mainly female centered families showed that emphasis was on using one's wits in preference to steady dull work with a dislike of formal intellectual and scholastic activities and an admiration of card sharks, gamblers and con artists as popular heroes. Such stereotypes, of course, do not give a true picture. There are many poor people who do plan for the future, and accept the standards and values of the middle class even if they regard them as a luxury and behave as if these standards didn't exist because they are out of reach.[10]

Kosa says that middle class families teach postponement of immediate gratification of wants for the sake of greater satisfaction later on (pain-pleasure principle replaced by reality principle). This makes possible planning for the future (career, marriage, family, financial) which helps to assure the acquisitive success. In seeking education, immediate gratification is postponed for the ultimate reward of a higher income and a better job later on. Being expelled from school or ending up in jail is regarded as a serious event in a middle class family where deviations are seen as having great future consequences (on career, reputation, etc.).

The lower class child constantly faced with concern for realistic basic needs tends to seek immediate gratification in all his actions and is likely to drop out of school, start sex earlier, drift into marriage (often because of pregnancy) at an earlier age (in contrast to college educated people who tend to marry later) and then experience marital instability and a broken home with an undue share of troubles, brushes with the law and school authorities and a higher rate of delinquency, mental illness and other social problems.

Such explanations have been refuted by observations that a poor drunk is more apt to end up in jail or in an alcohol hospital ward than a well-to-do one who more often has friends or family to "rescue" him. The poor delinquent child similarly is more apt to be expelled from school or have a police record than a well-to-do delinquent who is more often rescued by his family and either "sent away" or taken to a psychiatrist. The unmarried poor girl is less able to get an abortion when pregnant and less often able to get married and consequently less able to escape from her situation. Personality, attitudinal and behavioral differences are the result of poverty rather than an inherent characteristic of the poor.[11]

The common behavior responses that Oscar Lewis described in the Mexican poor as typical of the culture of poverty, were thought to be passed down from one generation to the next. He claimed that by the time children were six or seven they have usually absorbed the basic attitudes and values of their subculture and thereafter are psychologically unable to take advantage of changing conditions or opportunities that may present themselves. Much of this has been challenged by other sociologists and anthropologists who believe that these patterns of behavior can change. They are adaptive and can be abandoned when conditions no longer necessitate their perpetuation.

There is a higher rate of mental illness in the poor than in the rich. Eighty-five percent of studies clearly indicate that the rates of severe psychiatric disorders are highest in the lowest social classes—raising the possibility that mental illness may to some extent be a factor contributing to the development of poverty. In the Midtown Study[12] psychiatric symptoms reported by untreated persons indicated that the mental health risk of those in the lowest socio-economic group was greater than it was for middle and upper classes. They showed more signs of mental disorder or psychopathology, a higher portion with psychological impairment and a lower proportion of mentally healthy individuals. Their stresses were not much greater and it seemed that the lower-class persons reacted to stress more with psychiatric symptoms than others did. They seemed to have poorer defense mechanisms and poorer ability to cope with stress and life problems.

Highest rates of first hospital admission for psychoses, especially schizophrenic, were found in the deteriorated central city areas and the rates diminish as one moves toward the higher status suburbs. The possibility that this was a consequence of schizophrenics drifting into these areas was of course studied but the findings are contradictory.

Some studies found that schizophrenics were downwardly mobile in an occupational status and others that they were not. For example, Lapouse[13] and his coworkers studied first admissions to state hospital from Buffalo and found that the concentration of schizophrenics in the poor areas of the city was not the result of downward drift nor of migration into these areas. Hollingshead and Redlich[14] in their New Haven Study concluded that most of the patients they investigated who were in the lowest social class had lived in the slums all their lives. Only one percent of Social Class V schizophrenics in their study were downwardly mobile from their families and 85 percent clearly came from Class V families.

Dunham on the other hand found that individuals with severe psychiatric disorders seemed to show either disproportionately high rates of downward mobility or disproportionately low rates of upward mobility. He postulated that a selective process does operate in the downward movement of schizophrenics to a point lower than one's family of origin. He believed schizophrenics fail because they have an impaired ability to interact with their environments and fail to satisfy their own needs or to fulfill expectations of significant others or of society in general. It is possible therefore that schizophrenics either move into the less costly slums or that as an area of the city becomes a slum, the schizophrenics remain there more often than non-schizophrenics. It may be like the phenomenon described in low rent public housing project— where there is tendency for the unsuccessful to accumulate while the more successful move away. Over a period of time the housing project becomes a slum. If migration into the area does play a role in the high rate of psychosis in deteriorated central city areas, it doesn't involve foreign born as much as it does interstate migrants, both Black and White. The foreign born have lower rates of illness.[15]

Studies both here and abroad showed that unskilled workers who tended to be at the bottom of income and prestige scales had a higher rate of hospitalization for schizophrenia than other workers. In looking more deeply into this relationship, Dunham found that the average schizophrenic had a much lower occupational level than an educational level. He believed that while schizophrenics were able to complete their education they tended to fail when they entered the job market (because of premorbid aberrant attitudes, mannerisms and reactions which are obvious to others and keep them from getting a job or advancing when they have one). Failure to achieve success can in turn be an additional stress that may contribute further to the development of mental illness.

In the Midtown Study (which showed more psychopathology in the lowest socio-economic group) no single factor was found to be primarily responsible. It seemed that it was the cumulative effect of many factors, including deprivations and disruptions, that were experienced in childhood and adulthood.

Kohn suggests that the constricted condition of life experienced by people of lower social classes foster conceptions of social reality in their children that are so limited and so rigid as to impair their ability to deal resourcefully with problems and stress. In his opinion, this plus genetic vulnerability plus excessive stress could cause mental illness. The relevance of any of the three factors depend on the strength of the other two. If genetic predisposition is great, less stress may be required. If there is exceptionally great stress, less genetic vulnerability may be involved.[16] The unemployed have a higher rate for every type of psychiatric disorder and lower class Black males have notably higher unemployment rates.

While unemployment is a stress that may contribute to the development of mental illness—the findings of some studies suggest that some unemployment may also be the result of an inability to work or the consequence of less than optimum performance of a borderline (or mentally ill) individual who is the first to be laid off when business is bad and joins the ranks of the poor.

To suggest the possibility that there are genetic factors contributing to the higher prevalentce of poverty in minorities would in all likelihood result in the same intense objection that greeted the suggestion that genetic factors might play a role in the intelligence of different races.

At the 1976 Annual Meeting of the American Association for the Advancement of Science there was a demand made to end all research in behavioral genetics "lest it wreck the drive for social equality especially for Blacks and women." There is fear that investigators of a biological basis for behavior may confirm the idea that some of the inequities in society are based on genetic differences. Some geneticists claim there is convincing evidence that intelligence and behavior are determined (at least in part) by genes and that to think that there are no behavioral genetic differences between people is pure wishful thinking.[17]

To prevent research because the findings may disagree with someone's political or social leanings is remindful of past experience in the USSR. There was no hew and cry from social activists when R. W. Miller, Chief of the Epidemiology Branch of the National Cancer Institute was quoted as reporting that the incidence of cancer may be genetically influenced as well as environmentally influenced.

Ewing's tumor is virtually absent in U.S. Blacks and very rare in African Blacks though the incidence of all bone cancer is almost the same among Blacks as in the total U.S. population. Malignant tumors of the testes are markedly less frequent in American and African Blacks, strongly suggesting some ethnic factor. Multiple myeloma on the other hand occurs at a higher rate in American Blacks. Blacks of all ages were found to have higher levels of the major immunoglobins.[18]

No one objects if Blacks are credited with a very special sense of rhythm or coordination, but the mere suggestion by a geneticist that there might be an inherited difference in intelligence that could be studied sets off storms of protests and accusations of racism. Communist leaders in the USSR at one time found it politically expedient to insist that genetic factors could be altered by environmental ones and therefore genetic factors were not appropriate things to investigate, and were therefore forbidden.

It may be possible at sometime in the future to study genetic factors in behavior and achievement with less resistance and accusation of racism than is likely at the present time. It is the fashion today to attribute everything to the environment—to social and political and economic inequities rather than to factors within the individual himself—inherited or acquired.

There are significant individual differences that are not confined to matters of taste but extend to (and are derived from) fundamental biochemical differences that are modifiable only to a minor degree by the environment. "What we call 'the normal man' is largely a figment of our imaginations. Human beings vary naturally and innately over a far wider range than we ordinarily suppose" and it is ludicrous to assert that all people are equal. Differences in children of the same parents can be observed in infants and personality characteristics have been shown to persist throughout life.[19]

Raymond Moley said, "Real equality is not something to be decreed by law. It cannot be given and it cannot be forced. It must be learned".

Pope Leo XIII pointed out that "People differ in skills, health, strength and fortune and that this is not disadvantageous either to the individual or to the community."

Margaret Mead told a Justice Department Equal Opportunity Project in Washington that to assume "if you give people equal opportunity they can do all the same things with it is a sham and a hypocrisy of the worst sort that has been destroying an awful lot of people. What I want to emphasize . . . is the only way you give people equal opportunity is to recognize their differences."[20]

Hardin claims that (perhaps) "the most ardent support of egalitarianism has come from those personally involved in social service and philanthropy. The human degradation that constantly confronts a social worker would be difficult to face day after day if he suspected that manipulation of the environment would be powerless in the face of genetic predetermination. Frank acknowledgment of the social worker's prejudice—the word is used correctly—against heredity is found in a statement made a generation ago by a director of a New York training school for social work: "The notion of biological heredity and of innate capacity, as a determining factor, would have a paralyzing effect upon the young social worker, faced as he is with problems of maladjustments of various kinds. Without the hope and courage which the theories of social causation and social control give, no one could long endure social work." To this one can only reply with Thomas Mann's courageous words, "A harmful truth is better than a useful lie." If social work cannot find a firmer foundation than a noble lie, then so much the worse for it." Instead of insisting that all men are created equal, "we must learn to understand and to live with people who differ in many ways: in nose blowing, in sexual conduct, in ability to handle high-speed machines and meet emergencies, in liking for physical activity, in resistance to systemic poisons, in diet preferences and diet requirements, and in the most general sense—in taste. De gustibus non est disputandum we piously say. One cannot argue about taste. But the way to avoid disputes is not by denying real and ineradicable differences. Dispute must somehow be avoided even though we make full and frank acknowledgment of human differences. We must, in a deep sense, accept our humanity, our variable humanity. In the past we have not been notably successful in this, the moralists and the political scientists, who have, with rare and uninfluential exceptions, built their systems to fit only some fictitious "normal" man, and then have wondered why "men" did not behave like "Man." We will never solve the moral problems of men until we accept, in our bones, the insights of the biologist and the geneticist."[19]

There is a high incidence of mental retardation in the lower social classes but much of this, which in the past had been regarded as inherited, is now believed to be a pseudo-mental retardation that is secondary to the environmental deprivation that is associated with poverty. A majority of the mentally retarded are children of the lower social classes. They are thought to be retarded in function rather than lacking in basic endowment. In fact, social and economic forces are believed to be the most common causes of mental retardation in America.[20]

The wide differences in I.Q. among children in the different social classes are attributable by many to differences in cultural opportunity. If lower class existence does more often lead to functional retardation, it will be associated with more limited abilities to cope, to achieve economic success and a healthy mental state. Some of the poor then may be poor because of limited capabilities. They never acquire the skills that are required for success, and as a consequence have a higher rate of mental illness.

A Senate committee report estimates that 75 to 85 percent of the approximately 150,000 reported mentally defective and retarded children born in the U.S. each year are born in poverty. Whether these cases are the result of poor nourishment or social deprivation is not known. However, a spokesman for the Committee on Nutrition of the American Academy of Pediatrics put it well when he said, "There is no evidence that feeding people makes them smart. But it is undisputable that hunger makes them dull." Women poorly nourished in their own developmental period may not be able to provide the nourishment the fetus needs; it is possible the damaging effects of prenatal nutrition can operate for at least two generations.[21]

It is highly unlikely however that all men are born with equal intellectual potential, and that all differences are of environmental origin. All human characteristics are distributed along a normal curve. There are emotional and intellectual as well as physical differences in infants from the time they are born.

Garrett Hardin maintains that the censored truth of our century is that "all men are, by nature, unequal" and "we are as afraid of the consequences of admitting this truth as the Victorians were of the consequences of admitting that men are animals. Yet surely history will ultimately show that, in both instances, the consequences (of admitting this truth) are good and compatible with human decency."[19]

I do not want to be regarded as one who says poor people, and especially those on welfare, are sick, but on the other hand one must not ignore findings of studies, and of unpublished impressions of welfare workers, of the great extent to which there is obvious psychopathology in welfare recipients.

Sixty-seven percent of a heterogeneous group of welfare clients in the Washington Heights Section of Manhattan were observed and classified as emotionally disturbed.[22]

In Los Angeles County 60 percent of these receiving assistance from the Department of Public Social Services (DPSS) under the Aid to Totally Disabled Program (ATD) were in need of psychiatric services.

In the Santa Monica area of Los Angeles County, 60 percent of all the adults and children receiving welfare under the Aid to Families with Dependent Children (AFDC) program were thought to be good candidates for psychiatric help.[23] A large number of these who receive ATD have psychiatric disorders which are either the primary or secondary condition causing their disability, and many of those receiving "Old Age Assistance" are mentally disordered. In 1975, 30 percent of the blind and disabled adults awarded supplementary Security Benefits Income (SSI) were on the basis of a mental disorder. In children the percentage was double that.

Many women with dependent children and no husband are incapable of working because of some health impairment and although the extent to which their impairment and disability is psychiatric is not known, it is likely that there is a higher than normal rate of mental retardation, psychosomatic and personality disorders as well as psychosis in the group. In sickness surveys of pauper populations, mental disorders are frequently disregarded or overlooked.[24]

While much of the psychiatric illness and disability of welfare recipients may be the result of early environmental deprivation and social stress, when financial assistance is provided through one or another program (inadequate as these may be) it does not seem to appreciably improve the mental health of the recipients, many of whom still require help for a psychiatric disorder.

It is therefore a matter of speculation as to how much of the welfare problem is basically a psychiatric problem in a broad sense, that is not ordinarily recognized or admitted, and is dealt with as if it were just an economic problem. The failure of all welfare programs to achieve the relief they were supposed to provide may then not be the result of just insufficient financial assistance but partly a consequence of a failure to recognize and deal with a basic underlying mental health problem.

A significant fraction of the large number of patients who have been discharged from state hospitals to be taken care of in their communities has just shifted part of the responsibility from the department providing treatment to the department providing welfare. Dr. Jerome A. Lackner, Director of the State of California Department of Health, in discussing the problem of the chronic psychiatric patient, indicated that Social Security Disability payments permitted the transfer of life-support costs from the Mental Health to the Welfare System for hundreds of thousands of formerly hospitalized patients.

Sociologist Leonard Goodwin, of the Brookings Institute, points out that, "The background characteristics of the average welfare mother, which include only 10 years of education, three children, no husband and various chronic illnesses, do not encourage the hope that many of them can achieve economic independence.[25]

While there have been many studies showing a higher incidence of mental illness in the poor and in welfare clients, the extent to which psychiatric disorders contribute to the genesis and incidence of poverty have never been satisfactorily determined. To be sure, successful treatment and prevention of psychiatric disorders will have an effect on the number of poor.

Active treatment programs that have replaced the old custodial treatment of the mentally ill have helped many patients return to gainful employment and as further advances in treatment are developed, there undoubtedly will be many more. And, as the causes of the various psychiatric disorders are found, more effective preventive measures will be possible, thereby contributing to a further reduction in the incidence and prevalence of poverty.

REFERENCES

1. Davidson, J.: Politics and Policy. *Wall Street Journal,* August 27, 1985; p. 60.
2. Mall, J.: Children Vulnerable in Family Poverty. *L.A. Times,* March 10, 1985; Part VI. p. 15.
3. Nurth, Z.: Poverty up 52% Among Children. *L.A. Times,* March 23, 1985; p. 1.
4. *Women and Poverty.* U.S. Commission of Civil Rights, June 1974.
5. Lauter, D.: *L.A. Times,* April 16, 1991; p. A1.

6. *The War Against Poverty.* Brookings Research Report 107, The Brookings Institution, Washington, D.C., 1970.

7. Kosa, J., et al: *The Nature of Poverty,* Harvard University Press, 1989, Cambridge, MA, Chapter I; Poverty and Health, p. 26.

8. Eames, E. & Goode, J. G.: *Urban Poverty in a Cross-Cultural Context.* The Free Press, New York, 1973; pg. 222.

9. Ibid, pg. 225.

10. Kosa, J. et al: *Poverty and Health.* Harvard University Press, Cambridge, MA, 1969.

11. Ryan, W.: *Blaming the Victim.* Random House, New York, 1971.

12. Srole, L. et al: *Mental Health in the Metropolis.* The Midtown Manhattan Study, McGraw Hill, New York, 1962.

13. Lapouse, R. et al: The Drift hypothesis and Socio-economic Differentials in Schizophrenia. *Am J. Public Health.* 1956; 46:978–986.

14. Hollingshead, A. B. & Redlich, F. C.: *Social Class and Mental Illness: A Community Study,* John Wiley, New York, 1958.

15. Dunham, H. W., Phillips, P. & Srinvasin, B.: A Research Note on Diagnosed Mental Illness and Social Class. *Am. Social. Rev.,* 1966; 31:223.

16. Kohn, M. L.: The Interaction of Social Class and Other Factors in the Etiology of Schizophrenia. *Am J. Psychiat.,* February 1976; 111:117–180.

17. *AMA News,* March 8, 1976; pg. 4.

18. *Hospital Tribune,* February 16, 1976; p. 23.

19. Hardin, G.: *Nature and Man's Fate.* Rinehart, New York, 1959.

20. *L.A. Times,* September 15, 1976.

21. The Pregnant Woman: *Natural Business Woman,* March 1976; pg. 17.

22. Srole, L.: *Poverty and Mental Health:* Conceptual and Taxonomic Problems in Poverty and Mental Health. Amer. Psych. Assoc., Washington, D.C., January 1967.

23. Honig, M.: AFDC Income: Recipient Rates and Family Dissolution. *J. Hum. Resour.,* 1974; IX 304–322.

24. Inghe, G.: Mental and Physical Illness Among Paupers in Stockholm. *Acta Psychiatrica et Neurologica Scandinavia,* Supplement 121, Vol 33, Ejin ar Munsksgaard, Copenhagen, Denmark, 1958.

Chapter 4

SUBSTANCE ABUSE

During the past 30 years this country has experienced an enormous increase in substance abuse. This has been associated with dramatic changes in social attitudes and behavior and has likewise contributed to these changes. In spite of growing concern and increasing funding of interdiction efforts, substance abuse treatment programs, and education results have been disappointing. Although treatment has been effective for certain segments of the drug abusing population, these efforts have as yet had little effect on the overall magnitude of the problem. Those aspects of society that are associated with the development of the problem will require modification if an effective solution is to be accomplished.

While substance abuse has always existed, its history has been characterized by cyclical variations in the incidence and prevalence that at least to some degree has been related to society's attitude toward substance abuse. For example, during the Cultural Revolution in the Peoples Republic of China, drug abuse was sharply reduced if not eliminated, and alcohol abuse in Moslem countries has been controlled.

The incidence is also related to cultural changes (other than society's attitude). The current epidemic of drug abuse in the United States started in the late 1950's and 1960's and extended into elementary schools and colleges (LSD, marijuana and alcohol). The Vietnam War contributed to antiestablishment and free speech movements and to the availability of drugs (especially heroin and marijuana). Flower children, the sexual revolution, cults, communes, revolt against conventions and parental standards and beliefs characterized that period. That era was also characterized by political promises of the great society in which all needs would be provided. Welfare was enlarged with food stamps, and student loans, and was associated with emphasis on rights and entitlements.

Increased expectations were followed by disappointment and disillusionment along with anger and rejection of conventional standards of behavior. Societal, cultural and environmental factors would appear to be clearly associated with changing incidence of drug use.

The current concern about substance abuse involves fear of its effect not only on individuals but on society. There are many different kinds of drug abusers and the type and degree of worry about them differs.

There are patients seen in hospitals and physician's offices, including mentally ill and those seen for detoxification, the alcoholic wife or husband, the functioning person who drinks three martinis for lunch and gets intoxicated at social functions, the pilot or physician whose drinking puts others in jeopardy, the affluent cocaine user, the type depicted in the movies who gets drunk after some great disappointment, the drug users in prison, the homeless and street users and pushers who are involved in crimes and the drug war with the police, and the children in school who are using alcohol, marijuana, and experimenting with other drugs. Is the primary concern about their health or their effect on Society (the problem they create) or both?

Each type presents a different problem involving varying needs for treatment facilities, welfare and control and differing effects on the individual, his family and society.

Children in school who get involved with drugs and the more numerous poor drug abuser who is more apt (than the affluent person) to be involved in violence, crime, gang activity, wife and child abuse and the legal and welfare systems constitute the most serious problem. The affluent abuser is less inclined to use drugs intravenously and, therefore, less inclined to get AIDS, hepatitis or to overdose or constitute a burden to society and is more able to obtain treatment.

Legalizing drugs will certainly reduce the huge profit of the dealers that provides the fuel for the pushers and smugglers and will reduce arrests and overcrowding of the jails. But, as with alcohol, legalization is not the answer.[(1)] It can be expected to result in increased use—and we are left with the psychosocial problems created by the use.[1]

Treatment Programs have had little effect on the prevalence. Hayman[2] in his book on alcoholism stated "No mass disease of man has ever been controlled by treating affected individuals" and Berkitt[3] in an article in the Pharos recently repeated the same observation "For non-infectious disease, neither early diagnosis nor improved therapy has ever reduced nor is ever likely to reduce incidence rates." He added, "When tight boots are resulting in sores on the feet, it is of limited value to spend time treating the sores, unless the tight boots are replaced by looser ones. If a floor is flooded by a dripping tap, it is of little use to mop up the floor unless the tap is turned off. Medical students learn far more about floor mopping than about turning off taps—possibly because doctors can earn a lot more mopping than shutting off taps.

Reducing the supply of drugs is not the answer according to the American Medical Association (AMA) Board of Trustees.[4] In its report on *Drugs in the U.S.* it states, "Many Law enforcement and health officials agree that efforts to reduce the supply of drugs cannot succeed as long as the demand for drugs for the purpose of abuse occurs in a significant segment of society."

Treatment programs have had as little effect as welfare has in decreasing the prevalence of poverty or the availability of contraceptives in decreasing abortions. Diversion programs that have been so successful for airline pilots and physicians and AA detoxification programs for another special segment of society have not worked as well with the much larger number of substance abusers in the lower social classes who tend to be the chief target of law enforcement activities and government anti-drug campaigns. So it is necessary to look at the problem from another perspective and see if there are any preventive measures that can be employed.[2]

It is helpful to consider alcohol and other drug abuse separately, although most other substance abuse usually starts with alcohol use and often is complicated by alcohol abuse.[3] Alcohol use is legal and its effects can be titrated. While alcoholism is a greater problem than other drugs, it does not have the same degree of addictive potential. The use of alcohol by adults is not viewed as deviant as is in the use of PCP, Ice, heroin, cocaine ("crack") and social drinking is considered by most to be a normal activity in our culture.[4]

There is not the same concern about the conventional cocktail party as there is about social cocaine sniffing and heroin and crack use before dinner; clearly, it has to do with the intensity of the effect of the drug and propensity to addiction. Even if a gene that is associated with alcoholism (or other substance abuse) is discovered, there will be psychosocial determinants of drug abuse in addition to the genetic predisposition that will have to be dealt with if the problem is to be solved.

Cocaine and opiate use, although a smaller problem than alcohol abuse, is of greater concern because it is associated with crime, violence, prostitution, and AIDS and poses a greater hazard of addiction. Because of the large amount of money that is involved in the drug trade, children and gangs are more easily recruited as distributors and traders.

There is a clear relationship between the level of education, social class, and substance abuse. It is seen more often in the poor person, who is more often less well educated, a school drop-out, living in a female-headed household, in a neighborhood in which there is crime, violence, homicide, open drug-dealing and use, unemployment, prostitution and dependency problems associated with the welfare system. A disproportionate number of latch-key children, delinquents, abused and neglected children, teen-age pregnancies and school drop-outs characterize these areas.

There is a relative absence of good role models who could foster achievement, responsibility, ethics, morality and social norms.

Douglas Wilder, Governor of Virginia points out that "the only male role models many of our children ever see are those not working real jobs, but pushing and helping to push self-destruction in our neighborhoods. They have the jewelry, the cars and the girls."[5] Approximately 1 in every 4 young Black males in America is behind bars, on parole or probation . . . so many do not know their own fathers and 55.3% of Black families with children under 18 are maintained by the mother (most of them single).

Through identification or imitation these children are inclined to mimic what they have witnessed. They do not have the degree of control that adults do. They are more likely to become addicted if they use drugs. It will interfere with their education and maturation and future adjustment to society and their ability to support themselves and raise families. There is an increased possibility of their becoming a public charge and a liability to society because of illness, poverty, or crime.

The AMA Board of Trustees has concluded that "Understanding the correlates and risk factors associated with abuse of alcohol and other drugs is necessary for effective prevention, and research has identified these factors in children and adolescents that predict drug abuse: Poor parenting by parents who abuse alcohol and drugs; manifest marked conflict related to job, marital, health or financial difficulties; lack of closeness to children or involvement in their activities, ineffective discipline, and devaluation of educational achievement.

Children who fail in elementary school are more apt to become drug abusers. Use and social acceptance of drug use by peers, alienation from societal values, absence of religious belief, personalities characterized by rebelliousness, non-conformity, resistance to traditional authority and exaggerated independence all contribute. Current educational programs that just focus on factual information about drugs have virtually no effect on subsequent drug abuse.[4] Latch-key children are more likely to use tobacco, alcohol and marijuana and lower social classes are more involved than others in substance abuse and antisocial behavior.

Physical and sexual abuse in childhood have been found to be associated with later substance abuse and personality disorders. At the US Air Force Wilford Hall Medical Center, 46% of admissions who had been abused physically and sexually developed lifetime illicit drug use vs. 23% of those without any such history. 29% of the abused group were diagnosed as having personality disorders vs. only 3% of the non-abused admissions.[6]

Lee Robins[7] in her 30-year follow-up of a large sample of antisocial children concluded (as have many others) that problem behavior as a child strongly predicts problem behavior as an adult and that parent's behavior patterns are good predictors of their children's adult behavior. Sociopathic men pass their behavior patterns on to their children. Most of the antisocial children who were involved in theft, truancy incorrigibility, etc., had deviant family backgrounds, came from disrupted and often impoverished homes and had fathers who were sociopathic and/or alcoholic. They usually lived in lower-class neighborhoods where there were other children who were truant, stealing and undisciplined. As adults they had a high rate of arrests and imprisonment, poor occupational and personal adjustment, extensive use of welfare services and excessive use of alcohol.

She concluded that since truancy and poor school performance are nearly universally present in pre-sociopaths, it should be possible to identify children needing help through their school records.

Gittlemen in a similar longitudinal study of hyperactive children found that substance abuse disorders followed the onset of conduct disorders in an overwhelming majority of cases.[8]

At a recent meeting of the American Association for the Advancement of Science (AAAS), a reported study showed that children who are abused or neglected are more likely (than others) to suffer from alcohol and drug abuse and mental disorder when they grow up and more likely to be unemployed and arrested as juveniles and in adulthood. The study revealed that the abuse of children is more widespread than is generally believed.[5]

A review of the Cambridge-Summerville Delinquency Prevention Project that investigated the effect of casework therapy on several hundred underprivileged boys and found that (30 years later) childhood conduct disorders and hyperactive children tended to develop adult antisocial behavior and substance abuse, which varied according to the neighborhood in which the boys were raised.[9]

James R. Stabenau of the University of Connecticut Department of Psychiatry found that antisocial personality was the strongest predictor of alcohol and drug dependence, stronger than family history of alcoholism. However, family history of drug abuse alone did significantly predict drug misuse in his subjects, aged 15–19 followed for 5 years. One hundred and thirty one of the teenagers he studied were the offspring of one or two alcoholic parents. Eighty-eight were children of nonalcoholic patients seen in the University Dental Clinic.

Three or four disorder behaviors such as being expelled or suspended from school, destroying property, playing hookey five days in a period of two years, running away overnight, and being arrested and seen in juvenile court were the strongest predictors of any substance abuse and dependence outcomes.[10]

Franklyn Jenifer, President of Howard University says improving schools is not the answer if environment is ignored. "The home and neighborhood environment play a significant role and our urban centers are clearly antithetical to learning. Too many of our young people grow up in homes in which disorder, neglect and often violence are the norm and where no importance is placed on the child's intellectual growth. Too many of our young people live in neighborhoods that rank high in every indicator of social ill and where the only dazzle comes from the gold jewelry and flashy new cars of the drug dealers. Even schools with fine programs can't reach these children."[11]

According to Jerome Jaffe more than 50 percent of urban heroin addicts come from single-parent families and others from two parent families in which relationships are disturbed.[12]

There is no doubt that childhood environment is critical. It contributes to antisocial behavior that is associated with subsequent substance abuse and childhood mental health is the greatest predictor of good future adjustment to life. The association between delinquency and substance abuse and the relationship of both to dysfunctional families is clear.

Efforts to control substance abuse have had only limited success. Some treatment programs (Alcoholics Anonymous, Methadone, Naltrexone) have been successful for certain segments of the drug abusing population. Educational and mass media campaigns increase knowledge about substance abuse, but their effectiveness in reducing use remains to be demonstrated. Controlling the availability and criminalizing the purchasing and use of drugs while having some effect, have had disappointing results.

In order to have any real impact on the broader problem of substance abuse, a preventive approach must be adopted which takes into account demographic, developmental and social factors. Unfortunately, we have no simple preventive measures like the fluoridization of drinking water for the prevention of dental caries, or the enforced use of seat belts to prevent automobile accident injuries, or warnings on cigarette packs to discourage smoking (while subsidizing the tobacco industry) or use of condoms to prevent contracting AIDS.

If drug use is a manifestation of a changing, some would say a deteriorating, society then it could be helpful to consider those things which are said to be contributing to the deterioration, such as: increasing heterogeneity and size of the population, poverty, racism, fear of atomic war, emphasis on individual rights, violence and sex on television, lack of religious training, capitalism, unemployment, corrupt government, poor education, the change from an agricultural to an industrial society and lack of blue collar jobs, working mothers, welfare, latchkey children and increased child neglect and abuse. These are the same things believed to be contributing to the increase in crime.

In 1967 at a meeting of the American College of Psychiatrists, Professor Harold Visotsky talked about the need for preventive as well as service mental health programs. Prevention was to involve programs against poverty, juvenile delinquency and social disorganization among other things. It was to be aimed at high risk groups and involved setting up high risk registers of unwed mothers, social isolates, school dropouts, unemployed, prisoners, children in foster homes, persons having repeated trouble with the law, alcoholics, chronic welfare recipients and battered children. A major portion of the proposed program was to be concerned with the disadvantaged socio-economic groups who were at highest risk and would involve the participation of organizations dealing with the development of economic opportunity, education, social integration and general health care.

He proposed measuring the effectiveness of his 6-zone State of Illinois program with a monthly determination of the rate of imprisonment, juvenile commitments, alcohol related arrests, homicide, suicide, violent events, chronic welfare cases, unemployed immigrants, school drop-outs and marital dissolutions. I believe he would now include substance abuse. He also advocated identifying disturbed 1st grade pupils and referring them for treatment with the hope that intervening at the school level would avoid later intervention in a psychiatric clinic.

Dr. Duhl at the same meeting also proposed that prevention of mental disorder should consist of lowering the overall pathology level of community and Dr. Gruenberg maintained that the structure of communities causes illness when the individual can't cope with the upsetting environmental problems.

The prevalence of drug abuse is to some degree an indication of the mental health of a community and its prevention will involve some of the approaches that are advocated for preventing mental illness. Substance abuse and crime are not only correlated but have many common causes. In the past sixty years, we have become a crime ridden, violent society with overflowing prisons, courts that are jammed, and criminals being released from jail in order to make room for other criminals. Young criminals in Austin, Texas are called minutemen . . . the length of time they spend in jail. Crime is choking the criminal justice system in Los Angeles.[13]

In cities, gangs are running rampant. Thousands upon thousands of children are running away from home, being violent in or dropping out of school or getting into trouble with the law. Even the suicide rate of adolescents has reached unprecedented heights.

It is heartening to learn that the Secretary of Health and Human Services has called attention to violence as a public health issue that affects our entire society. He claims homicide which has become a leading cause of death is linked to poverty, poor health, alcohol and other drugs of abuse and family breakdown. Among other things, he points to the need to end the stranglehold of alcohol and other drugs of abuse, and to establish and support positive role models in the community because too often children are learning behavior from only negative role models.[14]

Deinstitutionalization and the more recent understaffing in many major cities of the mental illness treatment system has added to social instability. It has also contributed directly to the substance abuse problem. Two thirds of psychiatric admissions to the West Los Angeles Veterans Administration Hospital are found to have substances of abuse in their urine.

A sizeable fraction of prison populations can be given psychiatric diagnoses, including personality disorders and substance abuse. A percentage of the welfare population can appropriately be given a psychiatric diagnosis. In addition to those with clear-cut psychiatric disorders, there are the retarded (culturally or otherwise) and unemployable because of personality or motivational reasons.

Grossly psychotic people are roaming the streets and living on the streets, in part because there is such a distorted emphasis on individual rights. It is likely that increased drug abuse is just one more manifestation of a society whose deteriorating mental health is being ignored.

Despite all the advances that have been made in the diagnosis and treatment of psychiatric disorders, people seem to be more anxious, more depressed, more hostile, more dependent and less able to get along with each other if one is to judge by the way they drive, the language they use, the music they listen to, the increased number of divorces, child abuse, rape and disintegration of families.

About one-third of the homeless are mentally ill and a large fraction of the others are alcoholics or other substance abusers. Albee states 6.4 to 23.1% of the population have a diagnosable psychiatric disorder, and if one included all persons with conditions, such as tobacco addiction, school learning problems and adolescent rebellion, it would constitute 50 percent of the population.[6]

According to a former president of the American Psychiatric Association, Elissa Benedek, 12 to 20% of all children and adolescents in the U.S. suffer from mental or emotional disorders, and there is danger that the current emphasis on biological causes may result in social causes like poverty, neglect and abuse being ignored. Five to 26% of school-aged children are said to be suffering from persistent and socially handicapping mental health problems. In the State of Washington, 6.7% of children in public schools had severe emotional disturbances due to abuse and neglect.[15]

Despite the introduction of sex education in our schools, our teenagers have the highest pregnancy and abortion rates in the western world. There is increasing concern about the many children born of cocaine addicted mothers. In 1989 one out of 5 women delivered in the Washington, D.C. General Hospital was a drug abuser. One hundred and one infants were left in the hospital by cocaine addicted mothers and many had a variety of developmental abnormalities. These drug exposed children are at a high risk for school failures, emotional disorders and vulnerability to failure later in life.

William Raspberry sees little improvement in drug use, especially in the minority population. He believes the solution depends on our willingness to reassert moral and ethical values of family, community and character. In his view, American teenagers are less healthy, less cared for and less prepared for life than their parents were at the same age, with their excessive drinking, drug use, reckless sex and wanton violence, all evidence of a cultural breakdown. He says, "Cultural problems demand cultural solutions. What needs to be taught is self-discipline, self-control, individual and civic responsibility. Government can't fulfill children's emotional needs—nor its spiritual and moral needs. Government has never raised a child." But we might add, government can do things that strengthen families and increase their ability to install these values.[16]

While long term trends in substance abuse are affected by changes in social institutions, such as families, school, churches and mass media, that can influence the development of self-control over impulsive gratification, the act of taking or not taking an illicit substance is an individual decision.

In taking the substance, the reward is almost immediate; while the value of abstinence is distant. Individuals differ in the degree to which they are influenced by future consequences and the value that they assign to intangible consequences, such as a clear conscience, education, approval of others, etc. With maturity the selfishness and impulsiveness of children change, and more emphasis is given to intangible and future consequences. The outcome of course will depend upon the individual's developmental experience and the characteristics of the subculture, i.e., traditional vs. street gangs, etc.

Ghetto residents live in tough environments, where survival demands cunning and toughness. Substance use is integrated into various lifestyles of ghetto culture. The street drug culture in the slum contains many types of users and lifestyles. Oakland youths may adopt a rowdy or cool operating style. Rowdy youths begin to sniff glue and use alcohol, mainly wine, during preadolescence. They stress physical prowess, violence, and delinquency. Cool youths, in contrast are of several types, including "mellow dud" and "pothead," and value control over behavior. Effective prevention must concern itself with these developmental and social influences.

Studies have demonstrated that antisocial personality, substance use, and criminal activity are related to family factors such as large families, absent parent, alcoholism in parents, etc. As with crime, there is evidence that the antecedents of substance abuse occur at an early age, and crime and substance remain strongly associated.

In a UCLA Brentwood study of 285 male veteran cocaine users, the pre-drug history revealed a great deal of early delinquency. More than one-half had been expelled from school, one-half had been drunk in school and many had been involved in stealing and violent behavior. One-third had run away from home before age 18. One-half admitted having carried weapons and 10 percent had shot another person. It was a group that seemed to be predisposed to antisocial acts independent of their drug use. Deviant adolescent behavior became more pronounced as they reached adulthood, and was manifest prior to starting cocaine use. Multiple drug use was common.[17]

One study of the family background of 756 male heroin users looked at family and parental risk factors in substance use or other life outcome. Larger family size, higher birth order, parental alcoholism and parental absence were found to have a cumulative negative effect on how young the respondents were when they first left home, when they first used drugs regularly, on their level of tested academic achievement and on the probability of juvenile detention.

Ethnicity (for example, Irish vs. Jewish cultured drinking patterns), heredity, childhood environment and personality type were related to subsequent substance abuse and alcohol related problems. In a core-city group of subjects followed for 30 years psychologically well adopted personalities seldom got involved in substance abuse. What did contribute was a father's alcoholism, parental marital conflict, poor maternal supervision, no attachment to father, no family closeness.[18]

Conditions for optimal psychological development of children require a large expenditure of time and attention by caretakers. Large family size, absence of parents, and substance abuse by parents have a negative impact. Alcoholic parents alternate between excessive laissez faire behavior when under the influence of alcohol and rigid rule-following when sober, resulting in inconsistent and inappropriate responses out of proportion to the child's violation of family rules.

Constitutional factors interact with early family experience to influence the early socialization of the child and the confidence that, under reasonable circumstances, the environment will be consistent, and approval forthcoming. An intact and affectionate family with consistent rules and discipline will be less likely to produce impulsive, poorly socialized children than broken or discordant families with cold or abusive parent-child interaction or neglect. To the extent these premises are true, they underscore the importance of focusing on families if primary prevention strategies are to be effective.

Although treatment and rehabilitation programs have been effective with special populations, solution of the problem will depend on the development of effective primary prevention programs. Existing primary prevention programs have included educational programs in schools and at places of work, mass media campaigns such as the "just say no" approach, and other such efforts to provide education and change attitudes. Through these approaches more people have become aware of the potential hazards of substance abuse, and although some changes in attitude occur, any significant reduction in substance abuse resulting from these programs has been modest or difficult to demonstrate. These educational efforts compete with massive advertising messages, which treat alcohol positively, glamorize conviviality, and suggest nothing about the potential consequences.

Although the importance of early family intervention has been apparent for years, such efforts have been weak in comparison to criminal justice intervention and even educational programs. For more than 25 years Senator Moynihan has been stressing the fundamental importance of the family. He wrote in 1965:

> From the wild Irish slums of the 19th century eastern seaboard to the riot torn suburbs of Los Angeles there is one unmistakable truth in American history: A community that allows a large number of young men to grow up in broken families dominated by women, never acquiring any stable relationship to male authority, never acquiring any set or rational expectations about the future—that community asks for and gets chaos.

Just as the transition from a rural to an urban society produced the wild Irish slums of the 19th century northeast, so did the migration between 1940 and 1970 of 5 million Black Americans from the rural South to the large industrial cities of the Northeast help produce our ghettos, with their self-perpetuating poverty and family disorganization.

The child born in the ghetto is more likely to come into a world of broken homes and illegitimacy; and this family and social instability is conducive to delinquency and drug use. According to the 1990 Census, only 27 percent of households consisted of a married couple with children. Only one half of married adults had children. Individuals living alone is increasing. Only two-thirds of children in California live with both parents. Almost one million children in California live with neither parents.

As far back as 1950, E. Franklin Frazier of Howard University had written, "as a result of family disorganization a large proportion of Negro children and youth have not undergone socialization which only the family can provide. Because the disorganized family has failed in its function as a socializing agency, it has handicapped the children in their relations to the institutions of the community . . . (and) has been partially responsible for a large increase in juvenile delinquency and adult crime. Since the widespread family disorganization among Negros has resulted from the failure of the father to play the role in family life required by American Society, the mitigation of this problem must await those changes in the Negro and American society which will enable the Negro father to play the role required of him."

The increasing poverty of women has important implications for the nurturance of children. The great majority of poor persons in the U.S. are White. In 1984, there were 23 million, along with 9.5 million Blacks, and 4.8 million persons of Spanish origin. Most of the poor adults were women. The number of Black females who will never marry has tripled since 1960 and is now 25 percent, three times the rate for White females. In 1960, the proportion of women who had not married by their late 30's was similar for Blacks and Whites. By the time of the 1990 census Black females outnumbered Black males in the U.S. by at least 1.5 million. The disparity is due in part to the death rate among Black men as a result of homicides: urban Black males face a 1 in 10 chance of being killed compared to 1 in 80 for White males. The availability of an appropriate marriage partner has also been affected by an unemployment rate of nearly 11 percent by Black men, and by an educational disparity. The number of Black men and women attending college in 1988 was 687,000 women vs 443,000 men.

The breakdown of the family among the impoverished is reflected in the AFDC program. When it was established in 1937, half of the children receiving AFDC had one or both parents dead. By the early 1940s the proportion had dropped below one-quarter, and by the early 1980s only a handful of welfare families were needy because of a deceased husband.

Most women who go on AFDC do so for short spells, but the bulk of AFDC expenditures are accounted for by women who have eight years or more. One-third of women who end one spell of AFDC return for another, and three-fourths of all spells of AFDC begin with a relationship change whereby a female-headed family with children is created. Although it has been found that increase in the level of welfare benefits produced "a modest upward influence on the proportion of female-headed families, this does not account for the magnitude in the change of female-headed dependent families in the past 20 years.

There is, however, a strong correlation between teenage motherhood and AFDC. More than 50 percent of the women who currently receive welfare checks in California had their first child as a teenager. Last year California had the highest number of births to teens in the nation, and its AFDC caseload has been increasing sharply. Almost 70 percent of California's 2.2 million welfare recipients are children, with welfare paying the bills for one out of six of the state's children. The AFDC population does not fit any stereotypes: it is 35% White, 30% Latino, 28% African American and 6% Asian. Although the cost is great, federal expenditures on children are only about one-sixth of the total spending on the elderly.

In summary, family disintegration and poverty clearly are important factors in the development of criminal behavior and substance abuse. Therefore, a primary prevention program to control substance abuse should include actions that strengthen the family and increase the likelihood that children will be exposed to consistent discipline and values that reinforce long term goals over impulsive gratification. This is not meant to suggest this alone is sufficient. It needs to be part of a comprehensive program that includes an effective criminal justice, interdiction and educational components.

With determined, persistent, expensive effort on the part of society, there are some things that can be done although they would not be very popular politically. A preventive program should focus on correcting the pathogenic influences in early childhood (especially of the poor minorities) that contribute to the development of the pathologic personalities that in turn are disproportionately associated with substance abuse. The influence of alcoholic parents, marital discord, neglect, poverty, poor education, destructive welfare programs, female-headed households and a failing criminal justice system must be neutralized or eliminated.

ENDNOTES

(1) In the Netherlands there is defacto decriminalization of personal use of heroin and cocaine with limited success (and of questionable relevance to the U.S.). The number of heroin addicts tripled or quadrupled since 1977. Most belong to ethnic minority groups. While the percentage of American youth who have used marijuana has steadily declined from 1984 to 1988, the percentage of Dutch youths has increased. Since 1976 anyone 16 or older can purchase hashish for smoking in coffee shops which increased from 30 in 1980 to approximately 300 by 1990. Possession, use of trafficking in cocaine is illegal and the number of cocaine dependent Dutch adults is still small. Heroin is mostly smoked and 40% of hard drug users inject heroin, cocaine or both. Methadone has been distributed from mobil buses in the Hague since 1978 and the number of clients increased from 70 to 400 in the first four months and to 1500 one year later. A similar program was started in Amsterdam in 1982 where some addicts sold methadone to buy heroin. In 1988 methadone syrup was dispensed daily to 6300 users. The low threshold drug programs had limited success in reducing crime and prostitution. Addicts seemed to use methadone, not to abolish drug addiction, but as a safety net when they were unable to secure heroin or cocaine. In Amsterdam there was not the usual link between drug abuse and crime. 92% of arrests in Rotterdam involved crimes unrelated to drug acquisition. Most opiate addicts had highly unstable backgrounds. 75% had not finished high school and most had lost their jobs. Most addicts had been criminals before they became addicts. The Netherlands government has concluded that legalization of heroin would not result in a significant decrease in criminality. 62% of the addicts on methadone maintenance in Utrecht would prefer to get heroin.

The Dutch approach has met with little success in the underprivileged and immigrant populations and it is probable that it would not work well in countries (like the U.S.) with more heterogenous populations[1].

(2) California governor Pete Wilson insists "our priority must be prevention or else we will quickly and tragically come to a time when we simply run out of hospitals, prisons and treatment centers. We will be compelled to practice the most repugnant but necessary fiscal and social triage — all because we lacked the foresight to see the obvious and the political will to avoid an avoidable future." It is better to recruit and train mentors for troubled youth now than to have to recruit and train more cops, more judges and more prison guards later. It is better to warn high school girls of the dangers of the drugs now than to try to cope with the hellish problem of an epidemic of crack babies later."

(3) Of 224 new alcoholic clients of an employee assistance program 90 or 40% reported having used cocaine; one third of them had used it weekly and one fourth monthly. D.C. Walsh, et al. *J. Stud Alcohol* 52:15–25. Jan 1991.

(4) The Public Health Service does not label alcohol a toxic substance that is habit forming as it does cigarettes.

(5) Thomas M. Maugh II reporting on the 1991 meeting of the AAS in the *L.A. Times.* 2/17/91, p. A-5.

(6) Comorbidity and multiple diagnosis bear on the problem of treatment of the substance abusers. In the Brentwood VA hospital over 50% of admissions in addition to suffering from a mental disorder are substance abusers. 76% of cocaine users have an associated mental illness (affective disorder, anxiety disorders, anti-social personality disorders and schizophrenia). By far the highest substance abuse rates, more than 83%, appeared among persons with antisocial personalities in a National Institute of Mental Health Study. Ignoring a mental disorder in substance abusers or a substance abuse disorder in patients with another mental illness is a critical oversight than can lead to a poor outcome of treatment. *Psychiatric News,* Dec. 21, 1990, p. 2. Nace and colleagues found that 57% of substance abusers admitted to a private psychiatric hospital had personality disorders. Nace E.P. et al., Axis II Comorbidity in Substance Abusers, *Am. J. Psychiat.* 148:1, p. 118.

REFERENCES

1. Schwartz, M.D.: Drug Reform: The Dutch Experience. *Hosp. Practice,* May 20, 1991, p. 93–100.
2. Hayman, M. & Thomas, C.C.: *Alcoholism.* 1966.
3. Burkitt, D.: Are our commonest disease preventable? *The Pharos Winter* 1991; p. 19.
4. A.M.A. Board of Trustees Report. Drug abuse in the U.S., *JAMA,* April 24, 1991; No. 16., Vol. 265, p. 2102.
5. *Wall Street Journal,* March 29, 1991; p. A-14.
6. Brown, G.R., & Anderson, B.: *Am. J. Psychiat.,* Jan 1991: 148:1, p. 55–61.
7. Robins, L.N.: *Deviant Children Grown Up.* Williams & Wilkins, 1966.
8. Gittelman, R. et al: Hyperactive Boys Almost Grown Up. *Arch. Gen. Psychiat.,* Oct. 1985; 42:937.
9. Report of the APA Task Force on Prevention Research. *Am. J. Psychiat.,* Dec. 1990; 147:12, p. 1701.
10. Stabenau, J.R.: *APA Psychiat. News,* July 5, 1991; p. 12.
11. Jenifer, F.G.: For Children at Risk, A Sanctuary. *L.A. Times,* January 27, 1991; p. M7.
12. Jaffe, J.H.: Psychoactive Substance Use Disorders. *Goodman and Gilman, Pharmacology Basis of Therapeutics,* Prog. Press, N.Y. 1990; Chapter 13. p. 643.
13. *Wall St. J.,* June 5, 1991; p. 1–14.
14. Sullivan, L.G.: Violence as a Public Issue. *JAMA,* 1991, Vol. 265, No. 21, June 5, 1991; p. 2778.
15. *42nd Institute on Hospital and Community Psychiatry.* APA, Oct. 1990.
16. Kids Need a Moral Compass to go Straight. *L.A. Times,* October 25, 1990; p. B7.
17. Paredes, A.: Personal communication.
18. Vaillant, G.: *The Natural History of Alcoholism.* Harvard University Press, Cambridge, Mass., 1983; p. 311.

Chapter 5

THE HARD CORE*

K en Auletta, a writer for the New Yorker became interested in the problem of poverty and wrote a book, *The Underclass*. It bore on the outcome of a Federal Manpower Demonstration Research Corporation program (MDRC) that was designed to assist long-term welfare recipients (The chronic passive poor), the hostile street criminals (often school drop outs and drug addicts), the hustlers who operate in the underground economy and the chronic drunk, bums, drifters, bag ladies and mentally ill who roam or collapse on city streets—who comprised the segment of society called the Hard Core.

It was financed to the tune of over $82 million dollars over a five-year period from 1975 to 1981 with the goal of helping their group to become self-supporting. Basically, it was a supported work program in over 21 locations across the country that provided counseling, training, a one-year paid job and supplementary assistance where needed. The idea was to get some long term recipients off Aid to Families with Dependent Children (AFDC) welfare, resocialize ex-addicts, ex-offenders and delinquent youths and to assist them into undertaking gainful employment and away from government handouts. It was a voluntary program that involved over 6,600 individuals—half experiment and half controls.[1]

The women in the program had been receiving AFDC for most of the preceding three years. Their youngest children were in school so they were not tied down. The average mother had been on public assistance for more than 8½ years.

The ex-addicts were over 18 and had been in a drug treatment program for at least the past six months. The delinquent youths were 17 to 20, had never finished high school and had not been in school for the past six months. The ex-offenders were over 18 and had been in prison for the past six months, half had been heroin users. They had been

---

*This chapter is based on my article "The Hard Core" that was published in the *Psychiatric Journal* of the University of Ottawa, March 1984; Vol. 9, No. 1.

arrested an average of more than nine times. All were not working and had little or no work experience. Ninety percent were Black or Hispanic.*

The program provided jobs such as building maintenance, daycare, construction work and manufacturing. Work was under supervisors who acted as teachers, role models, and helpers. Subsidized employment and support were guaranteed for a year. The goal was for the subjects to continue working outside of the program after that. What were the results?

There was no positive effect on the delinquent youths; criminal activity did not decrease and essentially, the only positive result was with older women (36 to 44 years) and older men who did end up earning and working somewhat more than the controls. Those women, however, who lacked self-confidence and had low tolerance for work stress and who regarded themselves as victims of circumstances, did poorly and continued on welfare.

The findings on the ex-offenders, ex-addicts and problem youths were most discouraging. They tended to drop out of their jobs after six to seven months and in the end they were the same as the controls.

Overall, two-thirds of the more than 3,000 who enrolled in the program didn't complete it or go on to unsubsidized jobs. A guaranteed job didn't reduce use in the ex-addicts or induce many eligible mothers on welfare to enroll.

These discouraging results were similar to those in the 1967 mandatory work-training program for all adult Aid to Families with Dependent Children (AFDC) recipients. Day-care centers were provided for small children, job training was provided, but the results were poor. Granted that there are many reasons for this, I would like to focus on one aspect of the problem, its origins, recognizing that it is a very complex issue with many contributing factors.

AFDC was originally intended for women whose working husbands died or were killed, but as time went on, it increasingly included children whose mothers and fathers were neither blind, old, disabled, sick, widowed nor between jobs and who, as far as welfare critics were concerned,

---

*It is the young Black male who has the highest rate of unemployment and the highest rate of violent behavior. He is said to be suffering from "institutional racism" which is defined as "the process whereby persons are systematically denied the opportunity for full participation in and benefit from formal and informal institutions on the basis of racial or ethnic membership." So, here was a program that offered special help: training, support and jobs.

had no obvious excuse to receive public charity. In 1949, 42 percent of the fathers of the AFDC children were dead. In 1963, the number had decreased to six percent. The program became increasingly Black and urban and involved women who were not married or whose husbands had deserted them. By 1974, the number of recipients grew to nearly 11 million and now is much higher. At the same time, society has been changing and, particularly the traditional family in America.

The number of households headed by a married couple living with children and other relatives, that was the rule, has dropped steadily and now with the increase in the number of working mothers, less than 10 percent of American households consist of a fulltime, stay-at-home mother, a father who is working, and minor children. In Los Angeles County, one in seven residents depend on some form of public assistance such as welfare, food stamps, subsidized medical care or general assistance. From December 1990 to February 1992, there was a 13 percent increase in Aid to Families with Dependent Children and a 38.4 percent increase in General Relief.[2]

As of 1979, in New York City, 75 percent of all children born out-of-wedlock in the last 18 years were on AFDC. One out of every four Black children was born to teen-age mothers, 85 percent of whom were unmarried and many were illiterate and unskilled. (Over 20% of all Black children were born to unmarried teenagers.) In 1979, 55% of all Black children in the U.S. were born out of wedlock into female headed homes. In Washington, D.C., the percent was 65, in Chicago almost 79 percent and in Harlem 77 percent.

Most of the AFDC women had children who were born out of wedlock while they were young and unfortunately these women were not well suited for motherhood because of their own upbringing or lack of maturity.[3]

Sociologists blame a persistent puritanical view regarding premarital sex for the rise in teen-age pregnancy and not allowing schools to teach and advocate contraception. However, the increase in sex education and availability of contraception and abortion have not decreased the incidence of adolescent pregnancy and it raises questions about their efficacy at least for this group.

By no means does this involve just the Blacks. In the past 26 years there has been a 250 percent increase in White teen-age mothers and a 50% increase in the Black teenagers. What has probably contributed is their greater sexual activity and willingness to take a risk and bear a child. In addition, there has been, according to socialists, a progressive decrease in the authority and power of nuclear family and in the extended family. Grandparents and uncles and aunts are not around. With increasing frequency, even mothers are not around. Agencies have come between parents and children have taken over standard setting from parents and now there is confusion about whether this is their responsibility or the parents. Courts force some children to attend schools away from their neighborhoods regardless of parental wishes. Welfare agencies are too ready to assume support of children while ignoring the fathers.[1]

Health agencies provide abortions and contraceptives without parental consent or knowledge. Sex education along with available abortion and contraceptives convey an implied approval of sexual relations in teenagers (out of a wish to avoid unwanted pregnancies and neurotic attitudes about sex). Girls tend to seek sex more aggressively than before in their wish for equality, but either forget or ignore the fact that they are the ones who get pregnant and are left with the responsibility for the children they bear.

At a conference held in October 1975, co-sponsored by the U.S. Department of Health Education and Welfare Center for Population Research, the National Institute of Child Health and Human Development, and the Planned Parenthood Federation of America, there was a general support for policies providing services offering the widest freedom of choice and assistance to adolescent parents and their children. Only one person raised a question about public reactions to freedom of choice decisions about sex and having children where the results of this freedom often places a burden on society.

A number of participants insisted there was no evidence that adolescent childbearing had adverse consequences and should, therefore, not be prevented. When one participant advocated supporting a social policy aimed at preventing adolescent childbearing as well as providing services, there was heated objection by some to any policy statement (other than support for services).

To some degree, the lack of responsible parents has induced schools and government to take over parental functions, but the approaches have been simplistic and have created their own bundle of serious problems. A majority of female school dropouts are because of pregnancy, with the vast majority of teenage mothers keeping their babies. One might ask, "So what?"

It has been established that aborting a girl's education because she is pregnant not only scars her emotionally, but involves a risk for the generations that follow. The income of the young teenaged mother is half that of those who first gave birth in their 20's, and if married, they are three times more apt to end up abandoned or divorced than those who have children later on. Families headed by young mothers are seven times more likely than others to be poor. Their children constitute a disproportionate share of those on welfare and contribute disproportionately to the criminal and mentally disordered segments of society.[4]

Some see racism as the primary factor which would explain why Blacks and Hispanics constitute such a disproportionate part of this Hard Core. Some blame the capitalistic system that is more concerned with profit than jobs. Unfortunately, over 50 percent of Blacks and Hispanics in a city like New York lack skills in an economy where only eight percent of all jobs are blue collar. With so many of them dropping out of high school (35%–45% in the U.S.), there are too many for the number of messengers, janitors, busboys, and maids who are needed, and the school system gets blamed.

All of these are undoubtedly contributing factors, but what tends to be ignored is the extent to which the end result is a by-product of the kind of upbringing these children had, with their emotional needs unmet—a lack of discipline, of habit training and education in disorganized families often headed by young, school-dropout, immature females who were reared in the same kind of poor environment they in turn provide for their children. These are the dynamics and they involve a vicious cycle.[5]

The relief check becomes the accepted source of continued support, and this in time gets converted into a feeling of resentment and being a victim. Without a more mature role model, it is not likely that the children will grow up with ambition, a work ethic or sense of self-reliance. As Oscar Lewis reported years ago, they absorb the self-defeating attitudes and are not geared to take advantage of opportunities that might present themselves as in the Manpower Demonstration Research Corp (MDRC) program.

If racism and economic injustice were solely responsible for the perpetuation of poverty and all that goes with it, why do not more Blacks, Hispanics and poor Whites and other ethnic groups turn to crime and/or welfare? While racism exists and undoubtedly contributes to the problems of Blacks and Hispanics and others, Howard Smith, a Black ex-addict who worked with a group in the MDRC program in New

York,* told students in his life skills course that blaming "whitey" can become a convenience. Attributing one's difficulty to external causes relieves a person of any personal obligation to reorient his behavior and does him a disservice. People may be victims of racism or a system but they may also be victims of broken homes, of years of dependency, and the quick solutions that are anti-social and lead to disaster. Those who want government to do more, do not want to look at the family disruption, out-of-wedlock births, teenage pregnancies and lack of a healthy childhood environment, etc., lest it decrease government effort and demand more of the individual. Or, they believe that the government's doing more will solve all the problems although they have gotten worse as government efforts have increased over the past 40 years.

The growth in Black female-headed families is of recent origin and not (as others claim) a legacy of slavery and racial oppression. It is possibly related to the mass migration of Blacks to urban areas where there is a high rate of joblessness in the Black men.[6]

Auletta observed that those who have never held a full-time job, never routinely got out of bed early in the morning, or followed a dress code, or said "please" or "thank you," ever taken orders or worked with others, and have none of the habits most people acquire early in life and take for granted, are least likely to be helped by a supported work program to get and keep a job, to stop using drugs or lead a law-abiding life.

Howard Smith sees children—particularly minority children—as the victims of a crumbling family structure. They have not had the benefit of the traditional institutions that teach what is good and bad; church, schools, and the family unit itself.

Raspberry tells how an unemployed Black youth standing in the unemployment line, when he had an opportunity to sell himself by a TV interview, dwelt on how he wanted to dress and live and never said a word about his aptitudes and experience or his willingness to work hard or learn a skill. Raspberry believes that many of the inner-city youngsters have no sense of what work is really about. They live in homes where income means a welfare check that is unrelated to any regular exertion. They have learned that it is possible to survive without working.[7]

However, there are youngsters with skills who want to work but cannot find jobs. Sometimes they are turned down because of the way they look,

---

*Auletta reported his observations attending the course taught by Howard Smith. The group of 26 trainees became "the narrative spine" of his book.

talk or behave. They suffer from never having anyone who was interested enough in or capable of, teaching them the things that would be helpful.

The sexual revolution has been associated with a loss of stigma in having babies out-of-wedlock and an increased tolerance of pregnancies by the girls' mothers. However, teenage mothers frequently feel deprived having to take care of their children and, as a consequence, neglect (or even abandon) their children who later have an excess of low I.Q.'s, school failure, behavior problems and illness.

As welfare recipients, their attitudes may vary from complaining about not being given enough to blaming the cheating they do on the welfare staffs for not catching them. They sometimes insist the welfare system is established and continued to give the welfare worker jobs. They complain that welfare takes more (the person's self-respect and pride) than it gives. There is no feeling of gratitude. They regard welfare payments as an entitlement that is equated with social security, unemployment insurance and farm subsidies. They resent and, therefore, blame the system and the lack of jobs (that they may not stay on, if made available). With the absence of any personal accomplishment, it is no wonder that lack of confidence is seen as the most common finding in the "underclass." Self-confidence cannot come from welfare and dependence.[1]

Following World War II, those who migrated from rural areas to urban centers, leaving behind their social institutions and familiar living patterns, found few jobs to their liking. What they found, according to Auletta, were social workers, doctors, counselors, psychiatrists, child-development advisors, family planning experts, family courts—all the helping professions with their organized altruism. The state supplanted the families who believed they were relieved of responsibility and perhaps incapable. The children lacked adequate role models at home and looked for them in the street.[1]

Historically, welfare was primarily a function of charitable organizations but it has now been made a function of government. The U.S. Government, however, has catered to poverty and not to what is needed to eliminate it. Any inequality is now regarded as an injustice. Raspberry calls the U.S. Welfare system "The New Indian Reservation" and claims that it traps many people in poverty. He says welfare should be regarded as emergency help and not a way of life. What was "charity" has been transformed into "a right" and any attempt to change this is labeled inhumane, racist, undemocratic and a destroyer of civil liberties. In fact, there is constant pressure to increase benefits to give more rather than less, and some so-called experts on the problem of poverty consider programs to be a success when more people are on welfare, when the amount of money they get is increased and when they are politically organized to demand their rights. Their goals seems to be equalization of income of all people, unrelated to their contribution or effort. In effect, they are promoting a class of permanent poor and what has been called, a "welfare mentality."[8]

They have been quite successful judging by the figures provided by the Director of the U.S. Census Bureau. In 1970, there were 25.4 million persons below the official poverty level. In 1981, there were 31.8 million. This increase took place during the very period when federal programs to combat poverty were greatly expanded. Chapman says that it is the dissolution of families that creates the added burden of welfare. Only two-fifths of single parent families headed by women receive any child support from the father, while 50 percent receive some form of public assistance. It is the single parent family that is the new significant factor in the growing welfare burden. It is not that they are any poorer today—they are only more numerous (as some argue) because there was no comparable trend in the far worse times of the Great Depression. It is divorce and abandonment of women with children that accounts for much of the flow into poverty.[9]

It is understandable that there should be concern about mothers with children who need help. Welfare is a humane attempt to assist the needy poor. An unfortunate by-product, however, is that increasing numbers of children are being reared in environments in which they absorb or are indoctrinated with an attitude that it is their right to be supported comfortably and that if they do work, it must be something they enjoy and provides them with a greater income than welfare payments.

They are getting a message from society that it is not only acceptable to be dependent and, to some extent, that there is no alternative, but that it is their right. One may wonder about how many of the families of the 50 percent of Black teenagers who are unemployed are and have been on welfare and whether there is some relationship between the two phenomena. Unfortunately, working at a job paying the minimum wage often leaves the person with less money for food and other expenses than welfare provides because of the high cost of housing, transportation, and day care for children.

There is a great deal of concern about the physical and sexual abuse of children but far less about what I label "emotional abuse" or "psychosocial" neglect and maltreatment, which is much more common. There are many parents who, as a result of their own upbringing, have emotional, mental or personality problems that make them incapable of providing the interest, supervision and moral guidance that a child needs to develop. They may lack interest in the child's welfare or future. They cannot provide the constructive attitude that the child will need to adjust to society. They may be too strict, too punitive and demanding or too permissive. Worse, they have no expectations for children to live up to. The emotional needs of the child are as crucial as adequate food, clothing, shelter and physical safety if scars are to be prevented. (This is not to deny that some children turn out to be successful in spite of/or maybe because of the emotional abuse they experienced in childhood.)

It would seem that any program that is developed to reduce or prevent poverty (and crime and mental illness) must deal with these factors that so clearly contribute to their increasing magnitude.

There is a vast difference between assuring people a chance to earn what they need and simply giving them what they need. The first leads to a sense of self-worth and pride that can be passed onto children, while the second produces what has happened to Indians on reservations.[10]

There are many who are convinced that the welfare system needs to be altered to place more reliance on self-motivation and responsibility. Programs should try to assure recipients the same balance of rights and obligations that non-dependent people face in their daily lives. They should be expected to work, if employable, to stay in school if young, to obey the law, and so on.

Raspberry says, "We are learning, at last, that the better we take care of people, the more helpless they become. More thought is being given to help people be more self-sufficient. Blacks of unmistakably liberal politics are telling me that they are starting to see our best-intended welfare programs as a snare that traps people in their poverty. Even mothers could work as aides at day-care centers so other people can go to work." He believes there would be an enthusiastic endorsement of a program that said, "Here's a job, take it or lose your benefits." What is needed is constructive intolerance.[10]

Looking at the problem from another perspective, Hausman and Lerman advocate focusing on correcting the failure of many fathers to live up to their child support obligations instead of on programs to get mothers to take part-time jobs to qualify for welfare (which has not worked).*[11]

There is a need to re-examine the entire subject of rights, and particularly, the extent to which emphasizing them has resulted in a diminished sense of responsibility. Special interest groups pursue their interests with an attitude of "society be damned." The emphasis on individual rights had led to a society torn by competing interests. Nathan, who is a professor of public and international affairs at Princeton University, insists what is needed is a real commitment by people in public service to enforcing higher standards of performance, ceasing playing-political games with their own biases that are contrary to public good, and accepting limits. In the welfare field it will stress work (for the good of welfare recipients).[12]

It is interesting that in communist China, (in 1978 prior to normalization of relations with the U.S.) individual rewards were geared to a person's effort and productivity, while in capitalistic U.S. there is concern with individual needs. Instead of producing a happy and healthy society, we have experienced increases in divorce, crime, emotional tension and anxiety, job dissatisfaction, conflict, lower birth rate, and changes in standards of sexual behavior, language, dress and work. Lasch, in *The Culture of Narcissism* alludes to the preoccupation with self and pursuit of comfort and happiness that characterizes the American culture today and comments, "A once rugged and resourceful America is now seething with a destructive oedipal rage, masquerading as the pleasure principle." Capitalism has evolved a new political ideology, welfare liberalism, which absolves individuals of moral responsibility and treats them as victims of social circumstances.[13]

No longer is any distinction made in the army between illnesses that are the result of an individual's misconduct (e.g those related to alcohol and drug abuse) and those which are not. Responsibility is now assumed for all and, with government assuming more and more responsibility for people, we have witnessed an increase in cults, unhappiness, depression, demonstrations, disobedience, arson, vandalism, rage, muggings and robberies.

The solution to the problems of the underclass will at least involve a resolution of the conflict over whether primary concern should be focussed

---

*A committee in Wisconsin that has been studying the problem recommends that even low-income absent parents should be required to contribute, although it may create some hardship for their present families if they are remarried. This is no worse than the sloughing-off of their first family.

on the individual's freedom to do as he wishes or on what is best for society as a whole.

In an address to the American Bar Association, Solzhenitsyn said, "The defense of individual rights has reached such extremes as to make society as a whole defenseless against certain individuals." It took a man who fled from a communist dictatorship to tell us that, "It is time in the West to defend not so much human rights as human obligations."[14]

The problem of emotional abuse of children must also be dealt with. What chance does the child have to grow up to be a self-supporting, law abiding, mature adult who started out with defective genes, or was born to a mother who had little or no prenatal care, was a school drop-out, was not married and did not want the child. She came of a poor mother who was either never married or was abandoned by her husband or divorced, was on welfare as long as she, the child, could remember, had no work experience, little education, was functionally retarded, disturbed emotionally, unstable and without any support from an extended family.

What chance does a child have with a mother who feels impotent, unable to deal with her depressing situation or to change it, has no interest in seeing that her child has a good education, no expectations for her child, gives it no guidance, neglects its needs and provides no good role model for the child to copy. The mother, herself, had been reared in similar environment in an unstable family. She does not help develop good habit training in her child nor does she provide consistent, normal discipline.

What chance does the child have who was brought up in a neighborhood with a mixture of cultures, where distrust and hostility prevailed—a slum area with poor housing, a high level of lack of skills and unemployment, many on welfare and inhabited by prostitutes, drug addicts and drug pushers, juvenile delinquents and criminals, pimps and deinstitutionalized psychotics, where the population felt victimized, segregated and were hostile toward the police, where there was no feeling of security regarding food, shelter or safety.

Compare this with the child born to two parents who were married, had good genes, a mother who had good prenatal care and wanted the child and provided a stable, caring, loving environment. The parents were older, had completed their education, were of normal intelligence, and had work experience. They felt capable and able to alter their environment if necessary. They were concerned with their child's future, provided guidance, habit training, and were supportive. They regarded educational achievement as important and made known their expectations. They provided a home that was attractive (within their means), were law abiding, working, provided religious training and insisted on ethical standards of behavior. They felt worthwhile and were reasonably secure and trusting in their attitudes.*

Attempts have been made and are being made to correct some of the external environmental factors that are associated with membership in the Hard Core: welfare support to reduce poverty, community mental health centers for emotional disorders, special appropriations and programs to fight crime, subsidized housing and housing developments, financial assistance for education, food stamps, school lunches, disability benefits, special training programs like (CETA) and (MDRC) getting after fathers to provide child support for children they have abandoned and training mothers for part-time jobs.

These have not been successful and will not be until the internal, intrafamilial factors have been addressed and what I have referred to as emotional abuse corrected by the provision of wholesome environments for infants and young children in which they can be exposed to all the interest, guidance, training and role models that are so essential for normal development.

Society can eliminate unemployment by providing jobs and requiring individuals to work. It can get rid of some violent crime and felonies that characterize our society, by adopting a more realistic approach that considers the needs of society with as much emphasis as the rights of the criminal.

To accomplish this some change in the political-economic system will be required (this is needed to first solve the problems of unemployment). This has thus far been resisted because planned economy and an egalitarian society will bring in its wake—other problems—primarily loss of individual freedom. I believe this in part explains why all efforts to deal with the problem have so far been failures. Society has been unwilling to pay this price.

But no matter how one looks at the problem—controls and change of some kind will be needed and it is precisely these that are being so religiously resisted. Educators believe the solutions lie in better educa-

---

*All of these children do not turn out all right and many of those reared in very bad environments do. There are certainly other variables involved.

tional facilities; social workers believe that family planning which involves sex education, contraceptives, and abortions are what is needed; Blacks look to integration as the solution; psychologists to courses for parents; democrats to socialism; republicans to free market and less restraints on capitalism. Some insist that all people are created equal (because the Declaration of Independence says so) despite all of the differences that exist between individuals (the result of genetic as well as environmental factors). Some insist that everyone is entitled to happiness—or the pursuit of happiness without defining who is to provide this or how they are to obtain it. It is interesting that the words "work" and "responsibility" do not show up anywhere.

William Jennings Bryan reminded us that there is need to acknowledge that everyone doesn't have the same abilities and skills. He said, "we believe as asserted in the Declaration of Independence, that all men are created equal: but this does not mean that all men can be equal in possessions and ability, or in merit. It simply means that all shall be equal before the law."

Maybe the marvelous technological advances we are told are coming will eliminate the work that is needed to maintain and improve the standard of living that we now enjoy and yet provide adequately for all persons—with no permanent poor. The technological advances thus far however, have been associated with an increasing number of poor, dissatisfied people who feel abused, victimized, and antisocial which makes me somewhat skeptical of the utopian existence that some predict is on the horizon.

Ashley Montague may not have been so far off base as was thought when he proposed licensing of parents. He recognized that there were many individuals who were having children who were grossly incapable of rearing them properly. If a license is required to be a plumber or a chauffeur or a barber, perhaps one should be required for the more complex and important task of rearing children. If this seems too radical, the least that should be done is to provide child-care centers that are staffed and equipped to rear those children who cannot be reared by those who are responsible for their birth. The Israeli kibbutz is a possible model. Good day-care facilities should be provided and in these settings, it may be easier to take care of educational needs and do a better job of preparing young people for jobs and a constructive life.

Governmental programs have had little success in reducing the number of long-term welfare recipients (the chronic passive poor), the hostile street criminals (who are often school dropouts and drug addicts), the chronic drunks, drifters, and mentally ill who roam the streets.

In recent years that has been a four-fold increase in families headed by unwed mothers, a marked increase in the percentage of out-of-wedlock births in teenagers and others, and of children living in single-parent households (especially Black), and increase in marital separations and abandonment of women with children. The poverty rate of female-headed families is almost 50 percent. More than half of all Aid to Families with Dependent Children is paid to women who were, or had been, teenage mothers who tend to be least suited for motherhood by virtue of their own poor upbringing, interrupted education, poverty, and emotional immaturity. Their children contribute disproportionately to the hard core.

Attributing the problem to racism, capitalism, poor schools, inadequate family planning and sex education, or lack of courses for parents, ignores the extent to which it is a product of unmet emotional needs of children, defective rearing, lack of constructive role models and simplistic programs that cater to poverty instead of eliminating its causes. Changing the political-economic system to eliminate unemployment involves a price loss of individual freedom that society is unwilling to pay. Technological advances which so far have not helped, cannot be looked upon as a solution in the future.

REFERENCES

1. Auletta, K.: *The Underclass.* Random House, New York, 1992.
2. Report of the Los Angeles Department of Social Services (Feb. 1992), *L.A. Times,* March 4, 1992; p. B6.
3. Brashear, D. & Sholevar, P.: "Pregnancy Seen in Teens Least Able for Motherhood." *Psychiat. News* 1982; p. 15.
4. Wallace, H.M., Weeks J., & Medina A.: Services for Pregnant Teenagers. *JAMA,* November 12, 1982; 248:2270.
5. Brill, N.Q.: Emotional Abuse of Children. *Am. J. Soc. Psychiatry* 1981; 1:2, p. 41.
6. Danzeger, S.: Overview. *Focus* 12:1, Spring/Summer 1989; p. 2.
7. Raspberry, W.: "It's the Right to a Job, Not the Right to a Paycheck." *L.A. Times,* September 21, 1981; Part II, p. 5.
8. Lynn, L.E., Jr.: A Decade of Policy Developments in the Income Maintenance System, In: *A Decade of Federal Antipoverty Programs,* Haven, R.H. (Ed), Academic Press Inc. New York, 1977; p. 73.
9. Chapman, B.: "Seduced and Abandoned: American's New Poor." *Wall Street Journal,* Oct 5, 1982; p. 30.

10. Raspberry, W.: U.S. Welfare System: The New Indian Reservation for the Poor. *L.A. Times,* July 25, 1980; Part II, p. 7.

11. Hausman, L. & Lerman, R.: The Trouble with Workfare. *Wall Street Journal,* April 10, 1981

12. Nathan, R.P.: Thoughts Toward a Neoliberalism in the 1980's. *Wall St. J.,* Oct 7, 1982, p. 28.

13. *Time,* January 8, 1979; p. 76.

14. McLean, D.: *Psychiatric News,* January 1979; p. 21.14. *Time,* Jan 8, 1979; p. 76.

15. Montague, A.: Second Thoughts. *Human Behav,* September 1975; 4:10.

Chapter 6

WELFARE*

The Social Security Program has succeeded in decreasing the problem of poverty in the elderly. Unemployment Insurance has helped
materially for persons who have lost their jobs. Aid to totally disabled
and Supplementary Security Income has assisted many others in need.
By far, the greatest unsolved problem is the wide spread poverty of so
many females who head households. The more children such women
have, the greater is the likelihood of their being poor. High school drop
outs, non-whites, unwed mothers, mothers with many children and women
who had not worked before getting Aid to Families With Dependent
Children (AFDC) were the ones who were more likely to depend on
welfare for long periods.

The AFDC program that was designed to provide the support needed
to take them out of poverty has failed to do so. Most of the recipients
remain poor, with payments barely enabling survival under very trying
living conditions. The children who are reared by these mothers in
impoverished areas disproportionately contribute to the crime, drug,
health, and other problems with which society is faced. For this reason,
solution of the problem becomes more imperative.

As the number of AFDC recipients has increased, and the cost risen
by 1988 to 184 billion dollars,[1] objection to the program has increased.
Use of words such as "disadvantaged" and "underprivileged" instead
of "poor" has been criticized as implying an entitlement to government assistance. Inequality becomes equated with injustice and there
is an implication that the poor have been denied privileges and ad-
vantages that are their right and that they have a legitimate grievance
against the rest of society. They are then regarded as not just in
need of help but entitled to be given income and wealth that is taken
from others.

---

*Parts of this chapter are from "The Problem of Poverty and Psychiatric Treatment of the Poor,"
Psychiatric Journal of the University of Ottawa, Sept. 1977, Vol. III, No. 3:158–161.

"Underdeveloped" and "less developed" nations, previously merely "poor" become "underprivileged" and as such are entitled to be helped by an affluent nation like the U.S., not just when they suffer catastrophes like floods, earthquakes, famine, or epidemics but whenever there is a disparity in the standard of living. It becomes a moral obligation. Socialists are not called "socialists," but "liberals" by the media which knowingly or not promotes this bias.[2]

Such redistribution of wealth or income to the poor is not considered a workable solution since there never is enough money from the wealthy citizens to make a significant dent in eliminating poverty.

In New York, the adoption of a generous welfare program was followed by higher rates of crime, juvenile delinquency, drug addiction, teenage pregnancy and alcoholism in the recipients than when welfare checks were less generous. When welfare provides more generously for his family than a breadwinner can, there is danger of self-respect crumbling while many poor who are too proud to go on welfare, preserve their spirits by working hard at low paying jobs."[3]

The U.S. Welfare system has been accused of being a chaotic collection of more than 100 programs that have evolved with complicated and counterproductive eligibility standards, benefit levels and responsibilities. Large numbers of poor receive no benefits and only a fraction receive cash payments. The system is said to sustain people in poverty rather than teaching them how to get out of poverty.[4]

Each welfare reform movement was propelled by a supposed breakthrough and each has led to disappointing results. Minimum income guarantees, education and training programs, workfare and others have helped some, but their effect has been insignificant.[5]

Charles Murray points to the observation that huge increases in welfare spending by the U.S. government has had virtually no impact on poverty. The percentage of the population living below the poverty line actually increased at a time when it could not be blamed on a sluggish economy.* He claims welfare programs undermine incentives to work and have had an especially devastating effect on young Black males and other minority groups.** He believes private charities and state and

---

*By 1988 according to the U.S. Census Bureau, the number of poor in the U.S. had increased to 32.5 million, or 13.5% of the population.

**While unemployment of black males, ages 16 to 24, dropped to 23% in 1990 (from 37% in 1982), the percentage not in the labor market rose from 25% in 1954 to approximately 37%. Some have worked in

local governments are in a better position than the U.S. government to determine who is needy, and that welfare be made available just to the handicapped and those unable to work or to find a job. Furthermore, if help is provided to someone, who is in need, by friends and relatives instead of the government, there will be a greater motivation to stop being dependent. For many, being obligated to a friend or relative is not the same as getting what you are entitled to from the government. It makes sense for a pregnant girl not to marry the boy when she can get the equivalent of the minimum wage on AFDC. To her, it is a short term advantage. She doesn't look ahead because she has not been brought up to do so.[6]

Murray points to a 300% rise in illegitimacy over a period of ten years—something no one seems to talk about when discussing poverty. He realizes that his ideas are politically unpalatable but hopes they will stimulate more thinking about the problem.[7] Putting himself in the position of a poor able-bodied working age Black or Latino, he would want a job and a chance to make a living, a school that would teach his children as much as they could learn and safety from crime. His children should be able to play in a public park without fear that someone was hawking drugs there, he would want justice when he was a victim of crime—(i.e. catching the criminal and imposing a meaningful penalty on him), access to basic medical care and long term credit if needed.[7]

He does not want (or need) AFDC for a daughter, day care centers for pregnant teenagers, or any other services that would make it easier for his daughter to ruin her life. He does not want a juvenile justice system that would tell his son that being arrested is a game in which he can outwit the law. He does not want food stamps to be available to his children—nor subsidized housing, contact with social workers and lawyers who tell them that welfare is nothing to be ashamed of. He doesn't want them in the same classroom with children who are disruptive or who mock them for trying to get good grades.

The schools to which he sends his children are terrible, catering to the very students who prevent them from learning and the law does a terrible job of protecting them from crime.[7,8]

---

the past and either quit or were fired. They live off relatives, girl friends, hustle, do drugs or crime. They are not saving for the future, marrying the women they get pregnant or supporting the children they father. Most are physically able to work but have not had more than a high school education. They have, for the most part, come from single parent homes, with teenage mothers, live in public housing and in neighborhoods with many others like themselves. Murray C., *Wall Street Journal*, March 4, 1990, p.16.

Others are very critical of Murray's recommendations. They see no conclusive evidence of a strong link between generous welfare payments and births, family disruption and persistent poverty. For them "the welfare system is an indispensable safety net in a dynamic society, serving largely as insurance against temporary misfortune."[9]

They would recommend the opposite: increase in aid in order to provide more comfortable lives for the poor. Labeth Schoar of Harvard University points to programs that have been successful in changing the lives of poor youngsters and their families. The programs, in her words, were comprehensive and intense, with a wide range of services, coherently flexible, and ungrudgingly delivered. The quick fixes, cheap short cuts and isolated pieces of service were no match, in her mind, for the complex, deeply rooted tangles of trouble that beset overwhelmed families.[10]

There is no agreement about whether the poor must change if poverty is to be eliminated, because they are responsible for their condition, or whether society with its injustices must change to prevent people being victimized into poverty. Do the criminal behavior, violence, drug addiction, alcoholism, sexual promiscuity, mental illness, and instability which are more common in the poor serve to perpetuate their poverty and support the concept of a "culture of poverty" that is transmitted from one generation to the next; or, are these behavioral characteristics their way of responding to an inhospitable environment and society? Should the poor be held responsible for their condition or should society be held accountable?

In the past, distinctions were made between the deserving poor and the non-deserving. In 19th-century England, prostitutes, thieves, and swindlers were put in the same class as beggars—people who were predators in the community and unworthy of support. The Social Darwinists, like Herbert Spencer, believed that poverty was the consequence of inherited characteristics and that it was the fittest who survived and prospered. The English Workhouse and the American Poorhouse and Asylum that existed as late as the latter half of the 19th-century to house the poor, also lodged the aged, the chronically disabled, the insane, orphans and women, all of whom were unable to support themselves and had no one to take care of them.

To those who believe that the individual is responsible for his own life, society has no significant role in solving the poverty problem.

Those who view the social system as the chief force in any individuals adjustment, do not hold the individual liable.[11]

Some welfare workers say that poor mothers deserve more support from society because of the hard job they have raising children in poverty. They complain that workfare doesn't value the work the women do in the home and that full-time homemaking and child-rearing should be considered work. They point to the United Nations agreement that the governments should count women's work at home as productive and include it in the country's gross national product.[12]

In California with its serious budget problem and 16 percent of the U.S. welfare recipients, attitudes about welfare are changing. More is being expected of those getting aid: attending school, and not having additional children. Unfortunately, jobs are not available for those who cooperate in job training programs and many who get jobs can't keep them.*[13]

Since there are many causes of poverty, there is no single solution, and in all likelihood, there is no program that will completely eliminate it. From Biblical times, helping the poor has been regarded as an obligation of society—both religious and secular and despite all of the complaining, there is little likelihood that the people of the U.S. will tolerate abandoning them.

President Reagan commented that "Many of these (assistance) programs may have come from a good heart, but not all have come from a clear head."[14]

While there have been a few small local programs that have been successes, and while government programs have helped some escape from poverty, most programs for a variety of reasons have been failures. The cash payments and other benefits have helped many people survive, but the goal of helping them emerge from poverty was rarely achieved.

The Work Incentive Program (WIN) provided jobs or training—but did not succeed because the jobs for which people were trained didn't pay enough to support a family and better jobs were not available. Special needs prevented some mothers from taking advantage of the program. They either lacked the education, transportation, child care, or were ill.

---

*Of 310,000 who participated in the job training program, 104,000 started working, but only 28,134 ended up with a job that allowed them to get off welfare.

The Omnibus Reconciliation Act of 1981 designed to strengthen work requirements ended up reducing welfare for those who were working—but also reduced the incentive to work. The average wage of working mothers in one half of the states gave less disposable income than AFDC gave to mothers not working.[15]

In Massachusetts, the Employment and Training (ET) Program claimed putting 50,000 welfare mothers into productive jobs, but after spending $240 million in state funds and $84 million in federal funds, the ET program was an utter failure. The percentage of mothers on welfare rose 22 percent between 1983 and 1987 (a period of economic growth), while falling in the rest of the nation.[15a]

In an editorial in the April 1992 issue of First Things, a monthly published by the New York Institute on Religion and Public Life, it is pointed out that a bloated and bureaucratic welfare system on which the government is now spending $184 billion per year has only exacerbated the problems of poverty. Although trillions of tax dollars have been spent on helping the poor, there are more poor people than ever and "compassion is becoming a dirty word." According to the Census Bureau, more than 30 million Americans are living in poverty—with the official poverty line being a cash income of $12,675 for a family of four. If all welfare benefits (food stamps, housing subsidies, etc.) are included, the government is spending $11,120 on every poor family in America.[15b]

There are locally developed programs such as the Child Welfare League of America MELD project, the Houston Urban Affairs Cooperative (UAC) and the Boston Alliance for young families that are helping teenage mothers to stay in school by providing case workers, medical services and child care.

One problem that is often encountered is how to keep the 15 to 33% of teenage mothers from becoming pregnant again within 12 months after the birth of the first child, and then being less likely to return to school or get a job. There is less stigma now for teenagers having children out of wedlock, adding to the problems of how to keep them in school or a job and increasing the responsibility of teenage fathers.

There are those like Lester Thurow, Professor of Management and Economics at the Massachusetts Institute of Technology who believe that "welfare is an essential ingredient in Capitalism and that without it, Capitalism cannot survive. "It is the immune system that prevents capitalism from becoming infected with the germs of too much inequality.

The problem is establishing the proper level. As with medical disability, a determination must be made about who is not able to work."[16]

Those who are critics of the welfare system are branded as mean spirited and insensitive.[17] They may be the ones who point to the 88 percent of the 33.3 million called poor by the census bureau because their income is below a given level, but own their own homes, and cars, have air conditioning and microwave ovens. They note that "poor" Americans are now far better housed, better fed, and own more property than the average U.S. citizen throughout most of the century.

The average "poor" American lives in a larger house or apartment than does the average West European. Most American adults living today had a parent or grandparent who was poor by current standards, yet their behavior and values transmitted to their children were middle class.[18]

Opponents of welfare can point to the disastrous effect of the well-intentioned U.S. assistance program to the Federated States of Micronesia after World War II. The U.S. Department of Agriculture feeding program eliminated the need for anyone to fish or farm and changed islanders who had been self-sufficient to people without skills or incentives to survive. After 38 years of U.S. policy discouraging any sort of economic development, nearly two-thirds of Micronesian wage earners now work for island governments funded by the U.S. Congress. Peace Corps volunteers exhorted the Micronesians to expect and demand more social welfare programs. Outside investment was actively discouraged. By applying U.S. poverty standards, the entire population became eligible for aid. U.S. educational policies emphasized social studies over vocational skills and threatened to create a large number of highly college trained Micronesians for whom jobs were not available. In 1982, government employees there went on strike until the minimum wage was doubled—and the deficits covered by congressional appropriations.[19]

We produced a huge bureaucracy, unemployment and a reduction of the country's indigenous economy. Health care has improved but alcoholism, suicide and stress-related illness has increased. Portable radios, Michael Jackson, and "Death Wish 4" have replaced their traditional culture.[20]

The many approaches that have been tried or suggested have thus far made no dent in the burden of social services—which in Los Angeles has increased by 25 percent in a period of 2 years. One half of the AFDC was for illegals while the legal immigrants pressured for increased help.

They in recent years generally come with lower skills than immigrants in the past, primarily because U.S. policy now emphasizes family reunification. More children and old people are being imported, rather than workers. The people who came in the 1950's had a higher level of education than the average native American and were able to adjust well. In the 1970's the skill levels began to decline and are now below native skills. The present day immigrants are more apt to land in the ghetto from which they have great difficulty emerging.[21]

Illegal aliens can slip over the border and receive free prenatal care. When their children are born in the U.S. (at taxpayers expense) these children become citizens and automatically can be enrolled for AFDC. The number of citizen children of illegal parents in AFDC in Los Angeles County alone, rose from 97,665 in February 1991 to 121,042 in November 1991.

In California, without any change in the welfare system or demographic trends, the ratio of taxpayers to recipients of AFDC is expected to drop from 6.21:1 to 2.94:1 in the year 2000.[22]

The explosive growth of recipients is in part the result of increased knowledge about the welfare system and the legitimization of dependency fostered by the welfare rights movement. The California Department of Finance has found that the number of tax receivers in California is growing faster than the number of taxpayers. It predicted that with the projected growth of welfare recipients, prisoners, secondary higher education students and non-welfare medical cases, by the year 2000, there will be eight-tenths of a taxpayer for each tax recipient. The AFDC caseload is projected to grow four times as fast as the state population over a four-year period starting in 1989. (California with only 12 percent of the nation's population accounts for 26 percent of AFDC expenditures nationwide.)[23]

The situation is especially distressing with children constituting 70 percent of the 2.2 million welfare recipients—one out of six of the state's children. As of December 1991 more than 50 percent of the welfare mothers had their first child as a teenager[24] and most couldn't read or write well enough to hold a job. Only 59 percent of adults on welfare were considered able to work. The remainder couldn't participate in the workfare program for reasons of health, transportation problems or children under age three.

While over one half of all recipients were off welfare within 12 months, half of them were back on the roles within 3 years. For many, welfare provided a better standard of living than holding a minimum wage job. A family of three receives a maximum of $694 a month plus $277 in food stamps. The earnings for a 40 hour week at $4.25 an hour are about $735 a month.[25]

While teenagers don't get pregnant in order to get welfare, once they are on welfare, the higher the benefits, the more likely they are to establish their own households (and less likely to make the effort to find a job). Those who do stay with their parents are more likely to have a second child. Unfortunately, there are instances in which teenage mothers can't get along with their parents and necessarily expose themselves to a life with a poor prognosis for success.[26] This has consequences for the child whose future intellectual capacity and emotional security has been found to depend largely on the quality of mothering it receives when it is young.[27]

Because 32 percent of women on AFDC conceive and have more children after going on aid, there has been increasing demand to freeze benefits. California's problem is greater than most because its high bene-fit level is believed to act as a magnet for some who are on welfare in other states to move to California. Seven percent of current AFDC recipients lived in another state within 12 months of obtaining welfare in California and half of them were on aid just prior to moving to California. They came for a variety of reasons and it cannot be assumed it was just to get California welfare.[28]

Proposals to freeze benefits to discourage recipients from having more children, are opposed by Catholic Church officials who fear it would force poor women to have abortions and support the claim that the poor are responsible for their lives and for the children they conceive.[29]

It is depressing to learn that, what to many seems to be a very generous welfare program, does not eliminate poverty. AFDC, the major program, plays an increasingly marginal role in helping the poor. Nation-wide AFDC guarantees have declined in value by over 40 percent in the past two decades, although increase in other support (e.g. food stamps) have offset this drop by about onehalf. There is special problem in California, where fewer than 1 in 10 AFDC families get a rent subsidy and recipients may be forced to spend up to 80 percent of their income for shelter.[30]

AFDC now covers less than 60 percent of poor children as contrasted to 80 percent in the early 1970's. The proportion of children who are poor has increased from 15 percent in the mid 70's to about 20 percent today. Welfare, it is said, leaves children impoverished and is a terrible way to help the needy. Peter Goldmark, Jr. President of the Rockefeller Foundation asks if we would rather pay the mounting price of welfare, criminality, wasted talent and widespread family and neighborhood instability, than foot the bill for a national system of government supported service jobs.[31]

It has been pointed out that a woman with two children living in Pennsylvania earning $10,000 a year (roughly $5.00/hr) is only slightly better off than one who does not work at all. While her disposable income would be greater she would have lost her medicaid protection.

For those who live in a world where the most visible are criminals and where government benefits seem to come to those who have eschewed traditional work or family patterns, only chumps work long hours at low pay. He who can game the system becomes a hero. The community condones such behavior and as a result women feel less shame if they bear children out of wedlock. Welfare is accepted as a natural and legitimate option to marriage or work and men often feel little responsibility to support a family.[32]

Such low income people who are resourceful consumers of welfare and other social services are not then regarded as passive, helpless and easily manipulated. One study found that nearly all welfare mothers supplemented their welfare checks with income from other sources, including work.

Opinions vary about whether there should be a mandatory work requirement for welfare recipients. In 1983, there was such a requirement instituted in New York City for welfare mothers with children 17 years or older. Of 600 mothers, only 446 were considered employable. More than half did not respond to requests for work (and were dropped from the welfare rolls). The city concluded that most of the women were already working. The findings were the same for mothers with children 14 years or older. It seemed that when welfare recipients take jobs, they rarely inform the welfare agency.[33]

The expenditures of welfare families is far higher than their supposed income. Bribing them to enter job training programs is not what many of these women really want. All the successive waves of welfare reform, from programs that pay people to train, to programs that force them to work, amount to little more than failed attempts to make people behave better. A national support system with earned income tax credit and children allowances regardless of need was seen as a more rational approach.[34]

Research studies published by the Brookings Institution emphasized "The importance of individual behavior in determining who stays poor and who does not, rebutting the argument that virtually all the problems of poverty can be traced to a decline in the number of good jobs." There has been an overall decline in the traditional family structures which has hit both poor and non-poor neighborhoods and it is the changing values of mainstream American Society that is contributing to the formation of an urban underclass—not welfare benefits.[35]

It was expected that a formal education would undo the negative effects of a total family environment upon a young child, and as a consequence massive Federal effort was undertaken by the Office of Economic Opportunity Act, which aimed at correcting the causes of poverty, concentrating on the young, and on education and training. According to the Brookings Research Report, "The War Against Poverty," the Job Corps Program devoted to education and training of youth with disadvantaged backgrounds was less than a great success. Many left the program before they had completed it. The number of enrollees dropped and many centers in rural areas were closed because it was considered that their results did not justify their cost. Job Training Programs which work well for persons with good employment records were found to be less helpful to the hard-core unemployed and ghetto youths.[36]

Studies showed that the Federal program of spending millions of dollars on special education for poor children to improve their basic skills in reading and arithmetic—made no measurable difference. It was of almost no help to the children who were below-normal achievers whom it was supposed to benefit. (This was not the "Head Start Program" which was designed for preschool children.)

"Psychologist Joy Frechtling, Chief of the National Institute of Education's Compensatory Education Division, believes that the learning deficiencies of low income pupils may be attributable to cultural factors over which the school has no control—such as the students' parents, their at-home reading habits and social exposure."[37]

Dr. Catherine Chilman studied the very poor—people with extremely limited employment skills, unskilled, and casual laborers; the chronically unemployed or severely under-employed; and persons who are apt to have less than Grade VIII education and who, for the most part, come from families in which lack of education, lack of steady unemployment and lack of adequate income have tended to be the rule for several generations. These are the families often referred to as the "hard core" poor.

Manners, appearance, speech and niceties in interpersonal relationships, that may be important in seeking a job, are not of primary importance in the hard-core poor who are struggling with reality problems and survival. Honesty, respect for private property and the feelings and attitudes of others are more apt to be middle-class values. It is likely that suggestions to help the very poor change their child-rearing practices and family patterns of behavior so that children will not be so adversely affected, amount to wishful thinking rather than advice that is practical or feasible.

Relatively few studies of the rural poor have been done and yet they make up about 15 percent of the population, with 50 percent having incomes below the poverty level. Also it is not known why some of the very poor manage to maintain themselves without public assistance while others can't achieve even a minimal level of economic independence.[38]

One person who tried to find an answer to the question was M. E. Ensminger who studied a sample of women from a high-risk population in Woodlawn (a Black community on the South side of Chicago) to learn what distinguished women who were on welfare from those who were not. The women were interviewed in 1967 and again in 1975. They were all Black and had a child in a first grade classroom in a Woodlawn school in 1967 and still lived in Chicago or a surrounding area in 1975. The aim was to examine individual characteristics that might help explain participation in the welfare program in a high-risk community: who stays on welfare, who moves on welfare, who moves off welfare and who does not participate at all.

She found little evidence to suggest a vicious cycle of welfare in the sense of "once in a welfare family, always in a welfare family," or that those who come from the South or a rural area were more apt to be getting welfare.

There was a clear relationship to length of schooling. Those women who remained on welfare had the smallest proportion of high school graduates. Poor health also seemed to be related to being on welfare, but it could not be determined if those on welfare were receiving assistance because they were ill or if they adopted a sick role in order to legitimize their failure (as was suggested by others) or if dependence on welfare leads to poor health.

Moving frequently was positively related to being on welfare as was being unmarried with children. The absence of a husband made a big difference. But all of these factors taken together accounted for only one half of one variance in welfare status.[39]

There seems to be no question that unemployment contributes to poverty yet our society has never insisted that there be an opportunity to work for all those who are capable of working, even at low levels. Rather it seems to prefer the easier approach of giving welfare, unemployment payments or other assistance, all of which have their demoralizing effects. An alternative is to require some people to work at jobs they do not like and this is unthinkable (actually almost taboo) in a society placing a higher value on freedom of choice than on work and productivity.

There is no simple answer to the problem of eliminating poverty. Abandonment of the capitalistic system and democracy could bring about enforced labor and a more even distribution of wealth. Dictatorships can prescribe size of families and requirements of parenthood, and thus try to eliminate the vicious cycle of poverty-promoting emotional attitudes and conditions which give rise to further poverty, but the price will be great for society as a whole. The problem will still not be totally solved because in any sociopolitical system, for whatever reason, there will always be some poor. Even with a generous welfare policy for the mentally and physically disabled, and the mentally retarded there will still be great differences in standards of living.

It would seem that any movement in the direction of economic egalitarianism will be at the cost of freedom, and that one of the prices that will have to be paid to eliminate poverty will be loss of freedom (which may partly explain society's reluctance to come to grips with the problem).

In reporting on the effects of social deprivation of the development of young children from disorganized slum families, Malone remarked about the tendency toward over-generalization regarding the poor in programs for the poor. Poor people, he said, are no less diverse and heterogenous than affluent people. There is a tendency to overgeneralize about the difficulties of low socioeconomic families being the consequences of their disadvantaged status in an affluent society, and of the social deprivation, accompanying growing up in a slum. While the provision of better opportunities is basic to any assistance program for the poor, service programs of all types need to be adapted to what is present in the poor—their families and there neighborhood lives (as well as what is missing or deficient).

He points out that children coming from the most disorganized group of low-income slum families unquestionably experience maternal and social deprivation, unpredictable environmental stress and inconsistent patterns of care. However, their delayed intellectual and social development does not come just from this deprivation but from the presence of other factors which tend to impede or distort development.

Malone observed that curiosity and initiative are often discouraged or punished. Mothers often make excessive efforts to control the children and promote their own uncertain authority. External danger and low socio economic family life contribute to the children's delayed development and behavior characterized by excessive imitation (to avoid rejection or harsh punishment) that has a self-protective quality and is a means of coping with stress in new situations. They manifest a narcissistic orientation and a type of heedlessness. Their low self-esteem appears to be a product of their experience with their parents and neighborhood. There is a general feeling of powerlessness and despair. Their families and neighborhood are devalued by society. Their parents may give the impression of being unable to deal with environmental forces or to achieve or produce or to be something valuable. They may transfer their own feeling of worthlessness to the children. Lack of consistent parent concern and protection by itself can prevent the development of self-esteem or self-respect. This may be exaggerated by the proclivity of parents to criticize them, and also their lack of success in their activities. Such children may become highly skilled at manipulation and may show precocious ability to deal with complex environments (giving the appearance of a pseudo autonomy) yet lack caution and disregard for their bodily safety (an expression of their feelings of unimportance). Malone cautions that these feelings should be considered when programs for the poor are being planned.[40]

The basic questions to be answered are: Is the poor person a victim of his own deficiencies? Are the poor less motivated, less intelligent, less responsible and lacking in ambition? Are they genetically inferior and incapable of surviving (or flourishing) in a competitive society unless specially provided for by a society that expects and demands less of them than of its other members? Or, are the poor no different from others and just victims of misfortunes of birth, location or other circumstances? It must be emphasized again that there are all kinds of poor, and generalizations are apt to be inaccurate, confusing and counterproductive.

The approach to the problem of poverty cannot be a single one because there are many different kinds of poor whose capabilities vary tremendously and whose needs are quite different. The woman with four small children and no husband to provide support presents a very different problem from the elderly man who is blind or otherwise disabled. The woman with the small children may be educated and capable of supporting herself and the children if some child-care program could free her from the responsibility to take care of the children. The woman with small children who is illiterate, unskilled, unsophisticated, of borderline intelligence, and a chronic invalid, without any significant organic disease, poses a totally different problem. Negative income tax is no solution for her. The probability is that she could not be "trained" to work (and if past experience is any indication of what will occur in the future), chances are no job could be found for her if she were trained. The problem in such a case may not be just economic. What will happen to the children if reared by such a mother who is impotent, a chronic neurotic, incapable of effectively managing her own life or that of her children? What if she continues to have more children, and thereby adds to the problem? In the future, society may insist on a much greater role in the rearing of children of parents who cannot provide proper role models, care and motivation.

The problem of poverty which involves many more Whites than Blacks somehow gets disproportionately focused on the Blacks because of their higher incidence of poverty and in time the problem gets mistakenly blamed on racial prejudice—which not only does not explain the greater amount of poverty in Whites but cannot account for all the poverty in Blacks. To attribute poverty to racial prejudice is to insure the failure of any program designed to eliminate it. Poverty not only varies in degree and type, but is multi-determined. All poverty is not confined to the blighted city centers. There is no one cause, and as a consequence there can be no one solution. Family attitudes, stability, intelligence, and personalities play important roles in the way the condition of poverty is met.

In a country where the majority of people regard themselves as poor, they can, through democratic process, succeed through legislation in obtaining for themselves a greater share of the gross national product. If this, in the long run, has secondary negative effects, with a lowering of the standards of living for all, they can again through the democratic process make the changes desired by the majority. The responsibility is theirs.

In other countries small minority groups have seized power and by decree and force brought about a redistribution of wealth and sharing of production. In the United States today, with the highest standard of living and affluence ever achieved in the world, it is unlikely that there will be such an involuntary distribution of wealth in the near future. Gradual socialization would seem to be a more likely possibility. If this takes place unless more in the way of contribution is required of those citizens who are capable of contributing, it is probable that the system will collapse.

It is of course, wasteful and destructive to have people who want to work but cannot find jobs. The elimination of unemployment should have the highest priority in any program to eliminate poverty. It should be recognized that one problem, of such an approach will be the inability of all to engage in jobs they like or want. Peoples' wishes should be complied with as much as possible, but when it comes to alternatives of either no work and support by others or work that is uncongenial or not wanted, there should be no question about the choice. If a person is offered work that he is able to do and refuses, he would deserve no support.

It is going to be necessary for society to decide if reward should be based on the amount of one's contribution and effort or one's need (as determined by oneself or by someone else). Is egalitarianism the answer? Should the janitor in a General Motors plant be paid the same amount as the President of the Corporation? If not, how much of a difference is reasonable and to what extent will the magnitude of the difference effect effort, motivation, and productivity, and ultimately the common good?

Is the solution to poverty the equal distribution of production to all? Should it be done by governmental decree or only with the approval of all who will be affected—the non-poor as well as the poor? Should the poor be encouraged by government to make and force attention to their demands (as was attempted in the OEO Program)? Should a religious charitable approach be used to get the non-poor to agree? Should the non-poor be approached by a non-religious ethical educational effort that will give rise to guilt about the existence of poverty? Should there be a renunciation of the competitive, capitalistic system and an adoption of a totally planned economy where individual freedom and desire are less important than satisfying the needs of all? Can there be something in between?

Some sociologists point with great approval and optimism to the small victories that politically organized poor groups have achieved through mass pressure (getting a city's housing authority to paint their buildings, achieving some rodent control by a rent strike, or compelling a landlord to supply more heat). Such things do little to solve the problem of poverty. They make living conditions somewhat more tolerable. Each success can produce more confidence to demand more. It does not improve the economic or educational prospects of an individual or help him to move from unemployment to employment or from a low level job to a better one. It does not change his social position or improve his skill or contribution to society or his family.

In the long run there must be dissatisfaction with a welfare system that is rigidly paternalistic—that debilitates rather than rehabilitates. There is much that is possible in the way of self-help. More could be expected from a system which emphasized participation of the capable poor in finding their own solutions to their problems or in helping each other. This should not involve the exploitation of the poor by those who are trying to achieve political power and social changes which are not openly or frankly acknowledged.

It may be that support will eventually be provided by society to anyone who needs it—because of illness and/or disability, unemployment, age—or other reason and that welfare programs will not be specifically identified as they are today. In many respects it will be a different society from the one we know today. However, it would be well to remember the words of Justice Louis Brandeis who warned that, "Experience should teach us to be most on our guard to protect liberty when government's purpose are beneficent . . . the greatest dangers to liberty lurk in insidious encroachment by men of zeal, well meaning but without understanding."

In 1760, Alexander Tyler, a British historian, wrote concerning the fall of Athens, "A democracy cannot exist as a permanent form of government. It can only exist until the voters discover that they can vote themselves largesse from the public treasury. From that moment on, the majority always votes for the candidates promising them the most benefits from the public treasury, with the result that a democracy always collapses over loose fiscal policy, always followed by a dictatorship. The average age of the world's greatest civilization has been 200 years. These nations have progressed through this sequence: from bondage to spiritual faith; from courage to liberty; from liberty to abundance; from abundance to selfishness; from selfishness to complacency; from complacency to apathy; from apathy to dependence; and, from dependency back again to bondage.[41]

REFERENCES

1. *Wall Street Journal,* Sept. 25, 1990; p. 18.
2. Kristol, I.: The War of Words. *Wall Street Journal,* June 11, 1987; Editorial, Pröf. of Social Thought. N.Y.U. Graduate School of Business.
3. Kristol, I.: *Wall Street Journal,* July 12, 1976.
4. O'Hare, W.: Separating Welfare Fact from Fiction. *Wall Street Journal,* Dec. 14, 1987; p. 22.
5. Butler, S.: Welfare, Workfare, Warfare and Saviorfaire. *Wall Street Journal,* Oct. 10, 1988; p. A9.
6. *Firingline.* TV Program with William F. Buckley, KCET Los Angeles, 5pm Mar. 3, 1985.
7. Alexander, C.P.: *Time,* Nov. 5, 1984; p. 58.
8. Charles Murray: What do the Poor Really Need? *L.A. Times,* Dec. 7, 1984; Part II. p. 7.
9. Welfare: Promoting Poverty or Progress? *Wall Street Journal,* May 15, 1985; p. 34.
10. *L.A. Times,* Oct. 9, 1988; Part V. p. 5.
11. Eames, F. & Goode, J.G.: *Urban Poverty in a Cross-Cultural Context.* Free Press, New York, 1973.
12. Prescod, M. & Schellenberg, P.G.: *L.A. Times,* June 16, 1988; Part II. p. 11.
13. Conniff R.: *L.A. Times,* Jan. 10, 1992; B7.
14. *L. A. Times,* Aug. 1, 1985; Part I, p. 15.
15. *Women, Children and Poverty in America.* Ford Foundation Report, New York, N.Y. 10017.
15a. Welfare vs Work: *Executive Alert,* July/August 1990; 4:4. p. 2.
15b. What Should we do About the Poor? *Wall Street Journal,* Apr. 14, 1992; p. A18.
16. *L. A. Times,* Dec. 20, 1987; Part IV. p. 9.
17. West, W.: *Insight,* Mar. 23, 1987; p. 72.
18. Rector, R.: Poverty in U.S. is Exaggerated by Census. *Wall Street Journal,* Sept. 25, 1990; A18.
19. Randy Fitzgerald: *Wall Street Journal,* July 12, 1985; p. 24
20. Dolan, C.: Micronesia Suffers From 40 years of U.S. Welfare. *Wall Street Journal,* Jan. 3, 1989; p. 1.
21. *Financial World,* Mar. 3, 1992; p. 31–32.
23. *L.A. Times,* Dec. 15, 1987; p. M7.
24. *L.A. Times,* Dec. 13, 1991; p. B6.
25. Paddock, R.C.: *L.A. Times,* Mar. 5, 1991; p. A1.
26. Goodman, E.: *L. A. Times,* Feb. 3, 1995; Part II, p. 5.
27. Cal Thomas: *L.A. Times,* May 24, 1985; Part II.
28. *Wall Street Journal,* Feb. 25, 1992; p. A18.
29. Bethell, T.: The Church Needs a Dose of Reality. *L.A. Times,* Mar. 1, 1992; p. M5.
30. Ellis, V. *L. A. Times,* Mar. 4, 1991; p. A1.
31. Corbett, T.: The Wisconsin Welfare Magnet Debate. *Focus* 13:1, Fall & Winter 1991; p. 19–27.

32. Ellwood, D.T.: The Origins of Dependency. *Focus* 12: 1, Spring/Summer 1989; p. 7.

33. *Wall Street Journal,* Editorial, July 5, 1988; p. 18.

34. Schiff, A.: Let the Poor Redesign Welfare. *Wall Street Journal,* June 12, 1991; p. A14.

35. Lauter, D.: *L.A. Times,* Apr. 16, 1991; p. A1.

36. *The War Against Poverty:* Brookings Research Report, Washington, D.C. The Brookings Institution, 1970.

37. Mitchell, G: Special Education for Poor has Failed. *L.A. Times,* March 19, 1978.

38. Chilman, C.S.: *Growing Up Poor.* Washington, D.C., 20201, U.S. Department of Health, Education and Welfare, Division of Research.

39. Ensminger, M.D.: *Welfare: Its Relationship to Social Origins, Personal and Family Characteristics.* Presented at First Regional Congress of Social Psychiatry, Santa Barbara, California, Sept. 6–9, 1977.

40. Malone, C.A.: *Psychiatric Care of the Under-Privileged.* 8: 2, Ed. Guido Belasso, Boston, Massachusetts, Little, Brown and Co., 1971.

41. Heaster, J.: Is Bondage to be the Destiny of America? *Kansas City Star,* August 22, 1982; p. 1G.

Chapter 7

INDIVIDUAL RIGHTS*

The Miranda rule has been blamed by many for the increase in crime. It is responsible according to its critics for protecting criminals at society's expense. It is seen as just one manifestation of the trend to emphasize the rights of individuals—a trend that has contributed to the multiplying of the problems of society. Clever lawyers defend confessed murderers by using technicalities involving the question of individual rights as in the case of a man who was sentenced to death in Georgia in 1973 for having tortured and killed six members of a family but on whom sentence has yet to be carried out. Although the Supreme Court ruled in 1976 that properly drawn existing death penalty laws could be valid, hundreds of people have been sentenced to death, but by 1991, only one had actually been executed against his will. Supreme Court Justice William Rehnquist claimed that the Court had allowed the application of these laws to be surrounded with so many delays and procedural complications that the will of the legislature could almost never be actually carried out. The efforts of state legislatures to combat crime were frustrated by those who were obsessively concerned with protecting the rights of convicted criminals or were opposed to the death penalty itself. This partly explains why society has been so unsuccessful in fighting crime.[1]

Even the attorney who defended a man who had murdered his mother, father, and grandfather can't understand how laws that are designed to protect innocent people can be twisted to free someone who confessed four times to a killing, once on national television. The attorney did what he was supposed to do to defend the murderer. After the California Supreme Court accepted his argument that the confessions were inadmissable because of violations of the Miranda rule and reversed the conviction, he said that having done his duty as an attorney he should then act as an individual citizen. He protested the U.S. Supreme Court's refusal to reinstate the conviction, stating that the decision was an exam-

*Much of this was previously published in the *American Journal of Social Psychiatry,* II. 2, Spring 1982.

ple of applying logic of the rule to the point of absurdity. Braeseke, the murderer, had been warned of his rights by the police but asked if he could talk "off the record." He then told where he had disposed of the rifle he had used. He was again informed about his rights and again admitted his guilt. In a CBS film interview with Mike Wallace on 60 Minutes, he said, "I came downstairs and walked into the family room. The family was watching the TV set with their backs to me. Then I started firing the rifle."[2]

In New York City, a senior high school student was shot to death while walking home after a prom. A 16-year-old, tenth grade drop-out found a lawyer and surrendered to the police, admitting he had accidentally shot the victim who was resisting an attempt to take his ring. In a few days, an accomplice retained the same lawyer and added his confession. In preliminary proceedings, a state supreme court justice ruled that the confessions could not be used as evidence because the defendants' lawyer had used poor judgment in allowing them to admit the crimes. The justice based his decision on the 1949 opinion of the Supreme Court Justice Jackson that "any lawyer worth his salt will tell the suspect in no uncertain terms to make no statement to police under any circumstances." Two new lawyers who took over the cases insisted that the boys's interest had not been protected because no deal was made in return for their confessions. There was no question here of not having read the suspects their rights.[3]

When courts go overboard in protecting the rights of criminals, society has reason to be enraged. Why should the criminal justice system ignore to such a degree the rights of victims and all of society?

Some people were concerned that John Hinckley would not be able to obtain a fair trial because he was seen by the entire country shooting President Reagan on TV. Is it reasonable to expect jurors to have no knowledge of the crime? Vermont Royster commented that some expect juries to be "empty-minded"—not impartial but ignorant. He pointed out that most of the time the emphasis is on a fair trial for the defendant, but not for the two parties in every trial, both of whom deserve fairness. The second party in criminal trials is society. "The rules of evidence, the procedure in the courtroom, the multiplication of technicalities to protect a defendant have become so complex that the rights of society have been nearly forgotten. There's a widespread feeling that it's becoming increasingly difficult to bring common criminals to account."[4]

No serious attempt has been made to measure the emotional trauma that is experienced by the victims of the crime epidemic: the lasting fears and the diminished quality of life. In a few places some consideration has been given to providing some restitution to victims for the losses they have sustained. Mostly this is at taxpayer expense rather than the criminal's.[5]

This sorry state of affairs is partly the result of judges not only taking over the function of a legislature (by handing down decisions that have the effect of laws) but not using common sense in the process. They seem to be leaning so far backward in insuring the rights of individuals that they are in danger of falling over and taking society with them. It is as if the courts are saying, "Society be damned." No matter how guilty an individual obviously is, he is not punished if there has been any, even insignificant, compromise with the legal technicalities that the courts themselves have introduced. Some would attribute the phenomenon to a swing of the pendulum from a position where there was great abuse of the rights of criminals (or of the mentally ill) and to assert that the change is merely a cyclical one that will in time correct itself.[6]

The California State Supreme Court, in a recent decision, supported an existing statute that says defendants in capital cases may not plead guilty without the consent of their attorneys. Ostensibly, this is "to guard against erroneous imposition of the death penalty and to prevent defendants from using the state to help them commit suicide." However, dissenting justices called the decision "exceedingly strange, illogical, and inconsistent" and insisted that a defendant who was not insane should have the right to plead guilty with or without the concurrence of an attorney. They said, "a defendant, found rational and competent, should have the right to plead guilty to avoid the ordeal of trial, whether his lawyer wants him to or not."[6]

California Governor Edmund G. Brown, Jr., attributed some of the difficulty the state was experiencing in trying to control the rising amount of crime "to the tradition in this country of supremacy of the individual. Government, meaning society, is subsidiary."[7]

Even in instances in which there is no doubt about who did it and how and where a violent crime was committed, society will spend huge amounts of money in lengthy trials and retrials and then, at great expense, maintain the criminal in prison, while the victims and their families suffer without restitution. There is some feeling that execution is a "more cruel and unusual punishment than the death the victim or victims experienced at the hands of the cold-blooded murderer who didn't want to leave any witnesses to his crime."[7]

Assaults on students and teachers in the Los Angeles City Schools escalated by an alarming 27 percent, but because of a state court decision, the hands of school officials were tied in dealing with the troublemakers. School officials cannot expel a student unless a full hearing is held, which must include witnesses and attorneys to do the cross-examining.[8] How times have changed! Again, the rights of individuals, regardless of consequence, are given a higher priority than the rights of society (in this case the other students and teachers). The complexity of the procedures that are required to get rid of known hoodlums who cause confusion and disturbances and display antisocial or violent behavior in schools, is so great that teachers and school administrators are inclined to tolerate them and accept the cost of putting up with them. This has the added result of teaching students that they can misbehave without fear of consequences.

The Attorney General of California, who was concerned about the overly permissive atmosphere in the state, bemoaned the fact that, although over 21,000 people had been killed in California in the previous 10 years, and although voters on two separate occasions overwhelmingly asked for a reinstatement of capital punishment, no murderer had been executed since 1967[8] (In April 1992, the first execution took place.) A juvenile court judge painted a grim picture of growing youthful violence in Los Angeles, of a "children's army, armed with revolvers and shotguns and devoid of empathy for their fellow man."[9]

Some years ago, I learned that skid row applicants for welfare in the Los Angeles Civic Center District Office could be searched upon entering the building. This was justified on the a basis of so many of the applicants being recently released mental patients, frustrated high school dropouts, or heavy drug users. If their rights to privacy could be invaded, why can't suspicious characters be stopped in residential areas and asked to explain who they are and where they are going? Individual privacy is treasured as a fundamental right in democratic societies. When it is applied to criminals it becomes a perversion of principle. It protects the criminal at the expense of society.

"When reporters sought to obtain the criminal arrest record of the man who was accused of the murder of the prominent Washington, D. C., physician, Dr. Michael Halberstam, officials of the Federal Bureau of

Investigation refused to release the information because it would intrude on the privacy of the suspect. Subsequently, it was revealed that he was an escaped felon who had been sentenced to prison four times and arrested at least 25 times." In another instance, "an employee of a mental institution was accused of raping a patient and it was discovered that he had previously been convicted of rape. Texas law denied the hospital a right to screen his arrest record before employment." In another case involving a custodian of an apartment house for women, it was revealed that he was a convicted rapist and burglar only after he murdered a tenant.[11]

The American Civil Liberties Union is credited with the continued protection of criminals so that their chances for employment will not be jeopardized. The ACLU, however, seems to be unconcerned about the rights of the victims (or claims that is a price one pays for democracy). A serious offender, by the offence, has breached his or own privacy; by protecting it, a risk imposed on the rest of society.[11]

Despite strong protests by civil liberties groups, a government commission in England recommended giving British police sweeping new powers to arrest, hold and questions suspects in order to deal more effectively with Britain's increasing crime problems.[12] But in California the State Supreme Court handed down a decision that shifted responsibility to the prosecutor to prove that a defendant would flee if released on bail. The state's attorney general claimed this decision would prevent judges from considering public safety when deciding whether to release defendants on their own recognizance. He contended that it would result in the freeing of dangerous criminals. In the past, it was largely up to the defendants to show they were unlikely to flee if released.[13]

Los Angeles County Supervisor Edelman, while recognizing the importance of protecting defendants' rights, insists that they be balanced against the rights of citizens to safety and security in daily lives.[14] Another official, who was objecting to the failure of courts to enforce the law that required jail sentences for offenders possessing or using a gun in the commission of their crimes, pointed out that not only are citizens afraid to venture out at night, but insult is added to injury when the perpetrators of these crimes are so often back on the street before the victim is out of the hospital.[15]

At the present time, teachers are being beaten up and classes are being disrupted. Violent crimes and senseless vicious crimes are increasing. Mentally ill persons who are out of contact with reality, and unable to make sensible decisions about their own need for treatment, are deprived of treatment because their right to refuse it must be protected. Thousands of psychotic individuals are discharged from hospitals and returned to their communities, often to the dismay (and fear) of their families, neighbors and others in the community. Teenagers feel free to get pregnant and have their babies with the knowledge that the welfare program will provide their rights to establish their own households. The identify of juvenile murderers is protected lest their reputations suffer in the future. A person can't plead guilty to capital crime he has committed without the permission of his attorney. Employers have no access to an individual's criminal record.

We are told that reliance on technicalities is to prevent innocent persons from being unjustly imprisoned and that protecting and freeing criminals known to be guilty is the price one pays for democracy. Individuals insist on being able to go wherever they please with complete anonymity and regard a national identification card as infringement of their rights. There must be a reason for such an increasing emphasis on the rights of individuals in a country with the greatest freedom in the world. Some people say they are afraid that any infringement on rights will be the first step toward their being seriously compromised or completely taken away.

Emphasis on individual rights has contributed to an attitude that one is entitled to a life that is free of any stress or deprivation. The victim of a misfortune tends to blame everyone except himself leading to the explosive increase in law suits and the United States gaining the reputation of being the most litigious country in the world.

Drunk drivers who get into trouble, have the right to blame the bar owners. If a newborn baby isn't perfect, the tendency is to hold the doctor responsible. The relative of a man who stole a car from a parking lot and got killed in an accident, sued the owner of the lot for failing to prevent the theft. Minorities are inclined to interpret any disappointment to racism.[16]

The Harvard Law School Coalition (of students) for Civil Rights claimed they were damaged by a lack of diversity of the faculty—there were too few homosexual, minority and women professors.

Prisoners on Death Row in San Quentin filed a suit against California, claiming the right to procreate by artificial insemination by having their sperm preserved for a woman willing to be inseminated. Their lawyer claims that even the prisoners' parents right to be grandparents would otherwise be denied. One of the plaintiffs had killed his 10 and 4 year old nephews after they saw him rape and try to kill their mother, who was his stepsister. Another shot and killed an entire family—a woman, her daughter and two grandsons in a murder for hire.

When a library tried to bar a homeless man whose behavior and body odor disturbed other library patrons, a judge decided that the homeless citizen was exempt from the rules of conduct required by everyone else. Civil libertarians also supported the right of a homeless person to offend and disturb takes precedence over the rights of society at large.[18]

A student sued the University of Michigan for the mental anguish he suffered after being given a "D" grade rather than the "A" he expected. A prisoner, punished for escaping from jail, sued the sheriff and two guards for letting him escape. Two fans of the Washington Redskins football team filed a suit contending that a crucial call by an official, that led to the team's loss, violated the rules and robbed them of their right to see a victory.[19]

Individual responsibility for whatever befalls someone is rarely considered or mentioned. People even expect to be protected from their own gullibility and unpredictable accidents.

Individuals are no longer as self-sufficient as they were in a less populated, agricultural society where their survival largely depended on their own efforts. Society is now more complex, more technological, and only a small fraction of the population is living off the land. People are dependent on thousands of others they do not know for food, power, protection, transportation, and for their survival, and as a result seem to be more anxious and fearful than when their standard of living was much lower, their lives and health more precarious, and their comfort less assured.

Increased dependence in this more complex society can be expected to give rise to a higher level of anxiety and readiness to anger that accompanies unrealistic expectations.

One may wonder if the fear of any infringement on individual rights is related to an unconscious wish to be taken care of and the recognition that to be dependent is to be controlled?

There is a happy medium at which individual and societal rights are both assured. For people to live together with reasonable harmony, there must be limitations on what anyone can do. Traffic lights impose restrictions but make for more orderly and efficient automobile transportation. Health department regulations regarding sanitation impose compromises with freedom. All laws and regulations involve some limitations which presumably are for the common good. Individual liberty always comes up against somebody else's individual liberty. It can exist only within constraints not always clearly evident.[20]

One can only hope that the current preoccupation with individual rights is merely a manifestation of a cyclical change that will shortly reverse itself and remain in the bounds of a balanced social system. The alternatives are frightening.

Tocqueville believed that the rights of individuals in a democracy were sacred, but feared that the obsessional wish to protect his rights would lead the individual to close up on himself and to oppose every infringement not only of the state or his neighbor, but of the truth, the good and the beautiful. If so, the democracies would not survive much longer than the paltry religions, philosophies and art of past eras.[21]

REFERENCES

1. *Wall Street Journal,* Editorial, April 29, 1981; p. 22.
2. *L.A. Times,* June 5, 1981; Part I, p. 1.
3. Open and Shut—and Open Again. *Time,* June 8, 1981; p. 42.
4. Royster, V.: Thinking Things Over. *Wall Street Journal,* May 27, 1981; p. 24.
5. What Crime Does to the Victims. *Time,* August 3, 1981; p. 29.
6. Hager, R.: State Supreme Court Restricts Right to Plead Guilty in Capital Cases. *L.A. Times,* January 20, 1981; Part I, p. 3.
7. Reich, K.: Brown, 20 chiefs Confer on Crime. Los Angeles Times, January 6 1981; Part I, p. 5.
8. Welkos, R.: Officials Raise Alarm Over L.A. Schools Violence. Los Angeles Times, January 16, 1981; Part II, p. 4.
9. Welkos, R.: Children's Crime Army Prowling *L.A. Times,* January 15, 1981; Part II, p. 1.
10. Skid Row Welfare Office: The Employees Call it "The Pits." *L.A. Times,* January 9. 1981; Part V, p. 1.
11. L.A. Times, *Editorial,* December 22, 1980.
12. L.A. Times, January 10, 1981; Part I, p. 1.
13. Hager, P.: Deukemejian Assails Revised Bail System. *L.A. Times,* July 19, 1980; Part I, p. 23.
14. Merl, J. & Johnston, D.: Moves to Cut Violence Made. *L.A. Times,* December 17 1980; Part II, p. 1.
15. Officials Call for Jail in Gun Cases. *L.A. Times,* January 14, 1981; p. 1.
16. Birnbaum, J.: Crybabies: External Victims. *Time,* August 12, 1991; p. 16.
17. Goodman, E.: Inmate Right. *L.A. Times,* January 10, 1992; p. B7.

18. Editorial, Libraries and License. *Wall Street Journal,* June 12, 1991; p. A14.
19. Why Everybody is Suing Everybody. *U.S. News and World Report,* December 4, 1978; p. 50.
20. Bean, W.B.: Editorial, *Current Medical Digest* (CMD), September 1973; Vol. 40, No. 9, p. 662.
21. Manent, P.: Democracy in America. *Wall Street Journal,* January 30, 1985; p. 25.

Chapter 8

DE-INSTITUTIONALIZATION

De-institutionalization is just one manifestation, or reflection of the widespread change in the American culture. A coalition of several groups had a special interest in eliminating involuntary hospitalization and treatment of the mentally ill. Their campaign was justified as a humane effort to protect the rights of the mentally ill who were seen as being locked up in institutions for custodial care with no real treatment. The inmates were seen as being obliged to adjust to their confinement and given strong mind-controlling medication to assist them in regressing to a passively dependant, apathetic, irreversible state. While in some instances this was true, in most institutions active rehabilitation was pursued and major efforts made by interested and dedicated staffs to discharge as many patients as possible to productive community lives.

Large numbers of mental health professionals had been trained with the encouragement and support of State and Federal government. Some (including psychiatrists) whose numbers had increased dramatically following World War II, joined the mixed group of mental health missionaries, anti-establishment and antipsychiatric segments of society in pressing for the elimination of state hospitals and the substitution of mental health centers which they could run and offer the curative help that they felt had not been obtainable in the State institutions.

The antipsychiatrists, who attempted to illegalize any involuntary administration of medication, and who in one place succeeded in outlawing electro-convulsive treatment that had proven its worth for so many seriously depressed patients, behaved like overnight specialists who acted as if they were knowledgeable. They gained the unsolicited support of the segments of society, like the Citizens Commission on Human Rights—a church of scientology related organization, and a part of the legal profession that seemed more concerned with the protection of patients' rights than their well-being.

Below the ground level of the demand for de-institutionalization lay the fiscal concerns of the State governments which were faced with increasing expense of planning and building more and more hospital beds and staffing and operating them after they were built. There appeared to be no end in sight and the proposals to transfer the entire problem to local communities was most appealing. It also provided the legal profession (which had also increased greatly in its numbers) another field of activity—participation in deciding who needed what kind of treatment.

In pressing for the closing of the State hospitals the argument was used that mental illness developed as a reaction to stress experienced in the community and that health was to be achieved by learning to deal with this stress more effectively. This could not be done while the patients remained in the mental institutions. De-institutionalization was to be their salvation. State hospitals were said to be keeping patients for slave labor—in their kitchens, farms, and laundries. It was claimed that treatment in their communities would not only be less costly but would achieve higher levels of adaptation. The need to keep building more and more expensive State hospital beds would be eliminated along with the huge cost of staffing and maintaining them. The community mental health centers (CMHC) which were replacements for State hospitals, it was said, could establish catchment areas where the factors contributing to the development of mental illness could be identified and eliminated.

Medication whose use in hospitals was condemned, now would alleviate their symptoms and make possible re-socialization, remotivation, rehabilitation, and employment. It would be a new era without snake pits, exploitation of patients or deprivation of liberty.

Patients were to be protected at all costs. It was the hidden costs to families and communities that were not considered. The rights of society to be protected from deviant behavior were regarded as unimportant. Society was expected to tolerate increasing degrees of deviant behavior as long as it did not endanger any lives. Traditional standards of morality were to be discarded.

Dr. John Talbott, a past President of the American Psychiatric Association, points out that de-institutionalization that resulted in "an unprecedented shift in the locus of care of the chronic mentally ill was achieved at tremendous cost. More than 50 percent of the nursing homes are now populated by persons with primary or secondary diagnoses of mental disorder; thousands of disturbed persons wander our urban landscape without housing, and legions inhabit welfare hotels, board and care homes and adult residences."[1] The shift to nursing home care is regarded by many not as de-institutionalization but re-institutionalization—a new custodialism replete with its own failure and shortcomings.[2]

Many of the chronic mentally ill who previously were in State hospitals working on their farms or in laundries, kitchens, and housekeeping services were a lot happier, functioned better, had greater feelings of self-esteem and worthwhileness and contributed more to their own existence than they do now in this so-called more humane "improved" modern system of treatment where help is hard to come by, where they are on their own and given low priority by the professionals in some of the Community Mental Health Centers who are more interested in those who are not as ill. A hospital bed often is not available when needed and with increasing frequency these chronic, rejected, displaced patients are ending up in jail.

Los Angeles Superior Court Judge Eric Younger writing about the price society pays for the anti-gun-control people insisting on individual rights to possess hand guns, points out that "ours is an anonymous urban society" and the "gun registration wasn't necessary in an era when everyone in a community knew each other." Now "crazy people are everywhere. Modern notions of civil liberties and fiscal considerations have combined to produce a population of very disturbed people in every city in America. The notion of local treatment alternatives for mentally incapacitated citizens is a cruel hoax. It is clear that the vast majority of dangerously impaired people are out there on the streets."

"The man who writes his Congressman to oppose a gun-control bill doesn't take PCP and therefore is not likely to envision his 12-year old daughter as having rattlesnakes in her hair. He probably won't try to shoot her but someone whose "rights" he has inadvertently protected may." Judge Younger proposes a social policy that will protect the rights of hunters and target shooters but also protect society.[3]

The CMHC advocates who originally advocated deinstitutionalization and Community Treatment programs supported the claim that not only would their program be better (more effective) but would cost less. Now they bemoan the lack of adequate funds and attribute their failures to it. Although originally subscribing to a system of gradually increasing assumption of financial support of the CMHC by the communities, they are now back to looking to the State for all or almost all of the support. They envisage a system of clinics, half-way houses, day-care centers, nursing homes, skilled nursing facilities, general hospital beds and residential facilities with operating budgets that would seem to exceed by far previous costs.

The asylum and sanctuary concept has been abandoned. There is little or no mention of therapeutic community. "System" is the by-word now. It is basically a non-medical system. It makes no promise of commitment to research or interest in developmental and familial factors nor in the neuro-endocrine, psychopharmacologic or neurophysiologic, bio-chemical and genetic frontiers that are showing much promise of changing our understanding and treatment of mental illness.

To what extent Community Mental Health Centers are functioning as human service centers is not known. There is considerable variation in how they are staffed and function from community to community and center to center. Physical disorders in a great many patients go either unrecognized or untreated. Many do not even have an examining room. They promise to dichotomize the treatment of sick people, separate psyche from soma, and give up all that has been learned over the past many years of the intimate relationship that exists between the two.

Leighton[4] points out that "across the last 200 years there have been a number of periods during which it was widely thought that the cure and prevention of mental illness were at hand. . . . all guided by what seemed at the time to be compelling new ideas." (Some examples are the moral treatment movement, the mental hygiene movement, and the child guidance movement.) They were sincerely humanitarian and were attempts to bind the scientific and humane together.

He points out how "as the several movements turned away from scientific guidelines, they turned toward intuition, mysticism and magic. Decisions became dominated by emotions, myths, and wishful thinking. Goals became more ambitious, more numerous—unmanageable and unrealizable. There was over-claiming and overselling." He quotes Dorothy Dix as having stated that "Insanity is as curable as a fever or cold." Leighton claims there is an underlying conceptual and emotional tangle made up of numerous theories at multiple levels of abstraction, many of them contradictory and all of them controversial, unproven and subject to being disestablished . . . those with serious, chronic disabling mentally illnesses have been made the victims of hasty, enthusiastic but unrealistic projects. (In the past, removal of teeth and tonsils, colectomy, high colonic irrigation, etc.)

What needs to be recognized is that providing high level care for persons with serious mental disorders is exceedingly difficult to do and requires individuals with interests, abilities and training and levels of dedication which are not common.[4]

Mills,[5] a former State Commissioner of Mental Health, admits that the most important motivation of deinstitutionalizing the mentally ill was money and that there was no evidence that money has been saved, nor has its value ever been assessed. "The practice is widespread but its effects are largely unknown." Mills attributes this in part to the social and legal origins of de-institutionalization rather than clinical. He believes the movement was rooted in ideology rather than methodology and "the discharge of many patients antedated adequate research evaluating or supporting that practice."

The State hospitals are now left with the patients who are the most severely disturbed, dangerous or totally incapable of caring for themselves. To an increasing degree, the patients who have been discharged are ending up in jail. The mentally ill are arrested twice as often as those not so classified and it appears to some that centuries of progress have been reversed with the treatment of choice often penal custody.[6] Gralnick makes these same points in an excellent review of the *Origins and Signs of Failure of De-Institutionalization.* He, too, gives some credit to the legal profession which has now undertaken with no training the determination of treatment of the mentally ill.[7]

I had previously related another problem of society's (crime) to the unbalanced emphasis on individual rights.[8] There is good reason to credit, at least in part, the deteriorated state of the treatment of the mentally ill to this same preoccupation.

A society that permits lawyers to ignore the rights of the victims while over-protecting the rights of the criminals (often through the use of technicalities) also ignores its own rights when overprotecting the rights of the mentally ill (while keeping them from receiving much needed treatment). Solzhenitzen warned the American Bar Association that "the defense of individual rights has reached such extremes as to make society as a whole defenseless against certain individuals."[9] It has been said that the mentally ill are dying with their "rights on." Thousands of psychotic individuals have been discharged from hospitals often to the dismay (and fear of their families, neighbors and others in the community).

The injustices that result from this current preoccupation with and emphasis on individual rights are justified as the cost of preserving democracy.

It seems that existing laws not only cater to poverty and crime (not to their prevention and elimination) but to mental illness. Emphasis in part is on accepting and tolerating the mentally ill, not as much on the prevention of mental illness. The current approach which is dominated by fiscal and legal considerations in effect is implying an acceptance of mental illness—a problem to be tolerated and adjusted to.

De-institutionalizing the mentally ill and giving up on State hospitals as a means of treating the portion of the population that is out of contact with reality or has lost control over their impulses is somewhat remindful of the approach recommended by "authorities" like Arnold Treback, Director of the Institute on Drugs, Crime and Justice at American University, for dealing with drug abuse. He believes the war on drugs has been a failure—just the way the anti-psychiatry activists believe that the State hospital programs have been failures. He advocates giving states the option of providing narcotics and other habitual drugs to addicts as one (of many) approaches to minimizing the problem. Accept the inevitability of the problem, view it as a natural (but usually peaceful) disorder of a democracy—not as a destructive personal habit of neighbors (that cannot be controlled) to be warned against.[10]

There are crippling limitations of mental illness that do not yield to current treatment methods. Apathy, withdrawal, submissiveness and passivity may not be the result of hospitalization as many have claimed in promoting deinstitutionalization, but symptoms of the illness itself.[11] Some of these incurable psychoses may well be considered psychic malignancies. To push patients with these conditions into communities with even less ability to care for them than the hospitals, would be the equivalent of discharging patients with incurable cancers without consideration of possible alternative sources of help—in order to protect their rights.

A program that presumably was in part developed for the protection of individual rights—has in many instances turned out to be doing the exact opposite. Chronic and seriously disturbed patients who formerly were hospitalized now are forced to seek help in facilities like nursing homes, board and care homes, adult residences, etc., where the level of treatment is seriously compromised. While hospitalization in the past was not thought of as a right, legislative provision for it in effect made it a right. So we are now confronted with a situation where not only are societies rights being ignored but where patients rights too have diminished under the false banner of being protected.

Families have had to assume responsibility, and in some instances when assisted by Community Mental Health Center programs, this has proven to be helpful in the rehabilitation of the patient. Such success is more apt to be with the less severely ill and less disturbed patients whose behavior is less bizarre and where contact with reality is less impaired. Such patients do not impose as much of a burden on families as those who are much sicker, more regressed, more bizarre, more out of contact and more out of control—but who despite the severity of their symptoms, were discharged from hospitals because they were not considered homicidal or suicidal and presumably were able to take care of themselves.

There have been instances in which admission to a private hospital under medicare has been denied by the hospital utilization review committee and discharge of patients against their own doctor's advice. Other mentally ill patients who seek voluntary treatment in governmental hospitals may be turned away because there are no beds available.

Patients without families are even worse off. Some very sick ones, because no alternatives existed, were placed in board-and-care homes, some undertook independent living in run-down hotels, boarding homes and motels, and some became street people living in hallways, boxes or culverts or frequenting missions. In New York City, a deranged homeless man has a right to shelter. He also has a right to no shelter and to live and shriek and defecate wherever he wants.[12] Many became clients of welfare and police departments instead of mental health departments.

The criterion of "least restrictive" treatment rather than "most appropriate and effective" treatment which was introduced to protect patients' rights has resulted in what can best be described as a new form of patient abuse. If the rights of society were given equal emphasis, mentally ill persons who are out of contact with reality, unable to make sensible decisions about their own need for treatment and constituting unmanageable burdens to families, unable to provide supervision or control of their disturbing behavior, would not be deprived of hospital treatment, as they are now, (because their rights must be protected).

A scientific approach to the prevention and treatment of mental illness as proposed by Leighton, in a society that is determined to find solutions and pay the price gives promise of providing better results than we are seeing today.

Paying the price will involve the reestablishment of facilities for the mentally ill that were eliminated because someone else believed their rights were being violated. It will involve getting rid of laws that have forbidden the involuntary hospitalization of patients who needed it. It will involve some concern for rights of society to be spared exposure to persons who behavior is so bizarre, frightening, and at times dangerous. It will involve relieving families of the turmoil of trying to take care of psychotic individuals who are out of control and it will involve a willingness of the public to insist on adequate financing of the program that will accomplish all of this.

Approximately one-third of the homeless are mentally ill. They are the strange acting people who talk to themselves and sometimes frighten people with the peculiar gestures and exclamations. In the past, most the them would have been institutionalized. A majority of the rest of the homeless are chronic alcoholics or other substance abusers. While some of them were the bums, vagrants and hobos of the past, others were formerly productive citizens who gave up after being overwhelmed by depression or anger so that they turned against themselves. They suffer from a wide variety of diseases and are appropriate candidates for medical as well as psychiatric treatment. It is a disgrace for the wealthiest country in the world to ignore. This is a pathetic picture which these homeless wanderers display to the rest of the population—especially since an increasing proportion are young people who have left their homes.

REFERENCES

1. Talbot, J.A.: *JAMA,* Vol. 251, May 4, 1984; p. 2250.
2. Goldman, H.G.: *Hosp. & Community Psychiatry,* Feb 1983; 34:129.
3. *L.A. Times,* August 15, 1984; Part II, p. 5.
4. Leighton, A.L.: *Canada's Mental Health,* June 1982; Vol. 30, No. 2, p. 2–5.
5. Mills, M.J.: *Intern J. Law and Psychiatry,* 1982; Vol. 5, p. 271–284.
6. Goldsmith, M.F.: *JAMA,* Dec 9, 1983; 250:3017.
7. Gralnick, A.: *Am. J. Social Psychiatry,* Fall 1983; Vol. III, No. 4, p. 8.
8. Brill, N.Q.: *Am. J. Social Psychiatry,* Spring 1982; No. 2, p. 5.
9. McLean, D.: *Psychiatric News,* January 19, 1979; p. 21.
10. Trebach, A.S.: Time to Declare a Drug Truce. *Wall Street Journal,* August 2, 1984; p. 20.
11. Lamb, H.R.: The Need for Continuing Asylum and Sanctuary. *Hosp. and Community Psychiatry,* August 1984; 35:798–801.
12. Leo, J.: The Lingo of Entitlement. *U.S. News & World Report,* October 14, 1981; p. 22.
13. Royster, V.: Thinking Thinks Over. *Wall Street Journal,* May 27, 1981; p. 34.
14. Hager, R.: State Supreme Court Restricts Right to Plead Guilty in Capital Cases. *L.A. Times,* January 20, 1981; PartI, p. 3.

Chapter 9

AMERICAN SOCIETY AND
THE WAY IT MUST CHANGE

The changes that have taken place in society have an effect on parents and in turn on their children. Families have been increasingly isolated from the institutions that have traditionally played a central role in family life and the socialization of children in this country. Because of urbanization and its strident anonymity and impersonality, the separation of work and place of residence, increased segregation by age, and the growing secularization of society, the family is less likely to receive support in its child-rearing responsibilities from the extended family, the neighborhood and community and church. Without outside support, it seems likely that the problem will increase in severity and that the rate of child abuse, crime, drug dependence, failure in school and other indications of our inattention to the problems of children and families will also grow.[1]

More and more mothers of young children are now working — a majority of them, full-time and licensed day-care centers and facilities can accommodate only a small fraction of the children who have no formal care between the time school closes and their parents return from work. Fifty-three percent of women who work outside the home have children under two and the number of women with children under 17 who are working continues to increase.

Some working women have formed groups to take turns in taking care of their children. There are many mothers with children who need help in making similar arrangements and providing such help and facilities if necessary would permit many of them to take jobs that are available. Others with small children who require support can be used as surrogates in daycare programs that will allow other women to work. Some can serve as house mothers (and some men as house fathers) in residential facilities that should be provided for those children whose success in life depends on their being removed from their parental homes.

Changes in child rearing practices, economic anxieties, loss of confidence and trust in government have been accompanied by marked changes in the character of Americans and in the way they behave toward each other.[1]

Instead of developing classical neuroses, more people these days are seen with ill-defined anxiety and dissatisfaction with their lives, or with behavioral disorders. There is more sexual promiscuity and emphasis on individual rights to gratify or have gratified all needs and wants. Christopher Leasch at an American Psychiatric Association meeting in Atlanta said, "that the ethic of self-preservation and psychic survival is rooted not only in economic warfare, rising crime rates and social chaos, but in the subjective experience of emptiness and isolation. It reflects the conviction that envy and exploitation dominate even the most intimate relations.[1]

A 1991 report of the Los Angeles-based Children Now organization described some of the terrible things happening to children. "In the last four years alone, California has seen a 41 percent increase in the youth homicide rate; a 42 percent increase in the rate of children placed out of their homes, typically in foster care; a 23 percent increase in the rate of young people who spend part of their lives incarcerated, to a rate more than twice the national average. Everyday in California, three young people are murdered, 12 babies under age 1 die, 174 babies are born to teenage mothers, 179 teens drop out of school and 306 babies are born into poverty."[2]

That something fundamental is happening "can be seen in changing attitudes toward virtually all the social institutions that have formed the fabric of our society. The churches, our schools, our legal system, our economic system, and even our government are all under attack and all seem unable to deal effectively with the complexities of life in present-day America. Even the family is losing much of its integrity and strength and the Puritan work ethic is being rejected. Anti-intellectualism, anti-professionalism, and anti-institutionalism are evident everywhere. There seems to be a growing acceptance of the idea that everyone is entitled to housing, income, education, health care, and to a certain freedom from personal risk.[3]

Frustration is inevitable with "the whole clumsy mechanism of government becoming increasingly alienated from the people, to whose needs it no longer responds.[4]

The cultural and moral efforts required to reconstruct the ethic of work, lawful behavior and family responsibility in our inner cities, according to the Institute on Religion and Public Life, lie outside the competence of government. Parental authority and habits of self-reliance must be strengthened. The Institute sees the churches as the only available institution to take the lead in achieving this and a growing number of clergy are now calling upon people to take moral charge of their lives instead of making demands for additional government funds.[5]

Richard Halverson, a Senate Chaplain, described our moral state realistically: "We demand freedom without restraint, rights without responsibility, choice without consequences, and pleasure without pain. In our narcissistic, hedonistic, masochistic, valueless preoccupation, we are becoming a people dominated by lust, avarice and greed."[6]

There are some who believe that mental health professionals are not only unconcerned about this change in our society but may be unwittingly contributing to it by treating any deviant behavior as an "illness" or an "addiction," including violent crimes, and excessive gambling, jogging, sex, work, eating and especially drinking alcohol. Seeing them as a medical problem allows the so-called ill people to avoid moral and sometimes legal responsibility for their behavior and often provides a refuge from accountability. Health and Illness have replaced good and bad. There is an increasing tendency to attribute alcoholism to heredity, when it may be a predisposition, not a cause. Alcoholics Anonymous and Gamblers Anonymous which help by persuasion are not medicine. Regarding alcoholism as an illness, some claim, reduces stigma and encourages the seeking of help and sympathy on the part of the public. The alcoholics, however, see themselves as victims and free of responsibility for their actions. Money which might otherwise be used for unemployed and disabled may increasingly be used for the ever-increasing population of the behaviorally ill."[7]

Enormous changes have taken place in public schools. The changes may merely be a reflection of the other alterations that have taken place in society, or they may be a contributing cause. Thirteen percent of 17 year-olds and perhaps 40 percent of minority youths are considered functionally illiterate. Less than one third know when the Civil War occurred and two-thirds were ignorant of Chernobyl. All the studies that have been done in the last five years show that kids graduating from American high schools are historically and geographically illiterate. Nearly half of a cross-section of high school seniors couldn't find the United States on a map of the world and nearly half didn't know which came first, the American Revolution or the American Civil War. Increasingly teachers are asked to provide a good education but also to address social problems of drugs, sex, violence, broken homes, and poverty. Even children of two-earners, middle-class couples can suffer from lack of attention because their parents lack the time and energy.[8]

A well-scrubbed disciplined class is a stereotype from a bygone era. High school students today are quite experienced with alcohol, drugs, and sex. Pregnant girls are seen in school corridors, others deposit their babies in school day care centers. Violence and graffiti are common. Teachers, not parents, are called upon to be the first line of defense. Most kids look to teachers for the support they don't get at home. With divorce commonplace, youngsters frequently careen back and forth between parents like shuttlecocks. Single parents and two-earner couples are often too fatigued at the end of the day to show much interest in what goes on in school. In Chicago, administrations make it clear that students should be held back only once, and then promoted regardless of performance." (It is why a diploma from high school is no guarantee of literacy.)[9]

In Milwaukee public schools, 70% of the students are Black. The average grade point average is a D+. Almost half of the students drop out without graduation from high school. A newspaper reporter who was a former teacher spent one week teaching English at a high school with a White enrollment of 43 percent. She counted it a success if she just kept order. Students routinely talked, walked around and some didn't show up all week. Only 2 of 15 students read a short story and only 7 out of 25 turned in essays (on time) that were assigned as homework. This could not be attributed to poor support of the school. Students in a near-by private school, where the cost per student was approximately half of the cost in the public school, appeared and performed much better. A 1987 University of Wisconsin survey found that 62 percent of the Milwaukee teachers wouldn't want their children to attend the schools at which they taught.[10]

Rita Kramer, a New York writer who visited schools throughout the country, in her book, *Ed School Follies,* observed that education was child centered. It was the teacher's job to interest the students, not the students' responsibility to buckle down and learn. Emphasis was on teaching students about themselves and their feelings rather than on the outside world. Education school theorists seem to think that their students are so fragile that one low mark, one discouraging comment, will turn a child into a druggie or a dropout. They are hostile to standards, the idea of competition, and grades, that they believe characterizes and divide children. Performance and learning shouldn't count because they elevate some children at the very expense of others. There is a philosophy of leveling and sometimes antagonistic to achievement.[11]

Recognizing individual differences in motivation, talent and goals would make possible a more realistic and relevant educational system that is not encumbered by violence and preferred catering to non-performers. Advancement should be based on performance to avoid the current practice of granting high school diplomas to those who stay in school for the required number of years but are still illiterate. The diploma qualifies them for jobs they are incapable of performing satisfactorily and may be used to support feelings of unfairness or prejudice when they are fired.

Doctors who reviewed five sex education courses concluded that they had little or no effect on reducing sexual activity, increasing the use of birth control or lowering teenage pregnancy rates. Nor did they delay children's first sexual experience. The data suggested that a classroom course cannot be expected to change sexual behavior—as it is now molded by television, motion pictures, and adult role models.[12]

Bruno Bettelheim pointed out that sex education in school is a reflection of adult anxiety about young people's sexuality and that sex education is impossible in the classroom. It begins the moment you are born. It's in how you are bathed and diapered and toilet trained. You don't learn about sex from parental nudity or by showering together. How you feel about sex comes from watching how your parents live together, how they enjoy each other's company, the respect they have for each other, not from what they do in bed to each other.[12]

One physician, who found that dispensing birth-control devices and advice did not work, proposed that teenage girls who have had at least one pregnancy and were therefore statistically at risk of future ones be paid $30 a month to avoid pregnancy. They would have to be willing to have a pregnancy test and participate in counseling. He claimed it would end up costing less, and, to save money, the girls would be bribed into using birth control.

Raspberry in reporting this, maintains that the problem is not contraceptive ignorance but that so many youngsters have given up on their future. This is especially so for those teenagers who feel trapped in poverty and may see having a baby emancipating them with the aid of welfare to which they would be entitled. To him, their indifference is a symptom of helplessness, like dropping out of school and using drugs. They need help in seeing that the future is in their hands and in obtaining the education and career training that can lead to secure and satisfying lives.[13]

One response to the current ego-centered mentality with its greed, crime, drug abuse, family disintegration, moral vacuum, spiritual emptiness, political and business fraud and threatened national decline, has been the development of the Communitarian movement, started by Professor Etzioni of George Washington University. It advocates some compromise of individual self-interest for the good of society and the community and the reawakening of values, responsibility and commitment as the solution to the political corruption and social problems (health care, homelessness, poverty, and crime) that are out of control. It would involve the sacrifice of small liberties for the sake of security and the balancing of rights with responsibilities. Individual rights have been stressed to a point where they hobble the work of the police and public health authorities.

Many voters, faced with alternative undesirable choices and feelings of powerlessness have stopped voting. Communication with their government representatives is either impossible or meaningless unless previously paved by generous contributions. With basic needs of safety, education, employment and housing not being met, neighborhoods have deteriorated and honesty and morality have disappeared from the political arena.[14]

President Reagan called for a balanced budget eight consecutive years without ever having proposed one. He taught Americans self-indulgence instead of the slightest sacrifice for the good of society or its future prosperity. Even the coddled and petted voter could respond to a politician who did not go whoring after popularity, who offered spinach instead of candy and who asked for respect instead of love.[15]

Etzioni as a senior advisor to the Carter Administration discovered "that it was impossible to get politicians to consider doing what was morally right instead of what was politically expedient—because of the influence of business groups and special interest lobbies that financed election campaigns. He proposed mandatory public service for high school and college graduates, expanded government day care and medical programs, moral education in all public schools, tougher divorce laws, tracing social contacts of people with AIDS, a ban on private gun ownership and campaign financing reform to limit the power of big money special interest groups.

He said, "In the 60's and 70's people became reluctant to make moral judgments—to say something was right or wrong. Everyone was entitled to individual choices and all values were equated as equal . . . If parents don't bond with a child, especially in the first 2 years of life, under most circumstances there's going to be hell to be paid . . . If you want children, you have to take care of them instead of buying another VCR." According to Etzioni, most people are so concerned about crime that they would readily accept the inconvenience of police checkpoints in drug-infested neighborhoods, a proposal vigorously opposed by the American Civil Liberties Union (ACLU). Not only does the ACLU object, but minority leaders are afraid that the rights and opportunities of uneducated minorities would be limited.

Communitarians are opposed to the politically correct movement in colleges that compromises free speech. It is morality and law and order that is sought in order to prevent further decay that can result in a political upheaval with a much greater loss of individual liberty. Etzioni claims that no political or economic renewal is possible unless attitudes are changed.[13]

Another exponent of the need for change says "romantic attitudes toward schooling produce passive unstructured classrooms filled with children who lack self-discipline." Marriage is often less an emotional bonding than a breakable alliance between self-seeking individuals. If the nuclear family continues to be dismembered at the same accelerating rate by the year 2008 there would not be a single American family left. Droves of women have joined the labor force with little attention to children left behind at home. He is not asking the women to stay at home but pointing to the need for someone to do the parenting. When people ignore rules and mores, it gives rise to disrespect and social disintegration.[11]

Children who are adversely affected early in life in dysfunctional homes and who need help can be identified very early in their school careers. They are the ones who contribute disproportionately to the crime, substance abuse, poverty, welfare and homeless problems.

In kindergarten and first grade poor performance and/or behavioral problems should be accepted as signals that examination of the child and the family and home environment is indicated. In some instances problems can be identified in children in nursery schools and head start programs. The argument would be made that in poor minority areas with a predominance of single female-headed households, neglected and abused children may be the rule and comprise a problem so large and unmanageable that it would be impractical if not impossible to confront. Educational programs for this is not the answer.

Since a majority of single women head of households started having children as teenagers, it would behoove the Surgeon General of the Public Health Service to call attention to the unfortunate consequences of teen-age pregnancies as she recently did with regard to alcoholism in launching a campaign against college drinking, (calling on U.S. beer companies to halt springbreak promotions).

Day care centers with trained, interested staff should be provided by local governments when otherwise not available to provide a wholesome, constructive environment for a pre-school child whose mother was incapable of furnishing it. In addition to helping the child develop normally, it would enable mothers when they had no other recourse to continue in school, obtain training or get a job when these alternatives were not otherwise possible.

When problem children are identified, procedures for evaluation of the home environment must be adopted and developed as a practical necessity for all communities. There are some parents, male and female, who by virtue of disordered personalities or disabilities are incapable of rearing children. As Ashley Montague pointed out, no license is required to become a parent. As a public health measure, children, contrary to what one may wish, must be removed from traumatic, defect-producing environments, and cared for and reared in homes or asylums that are licensed and run by caring, trained parental substitutes who are interested in and capable of doing the job. That such facilities are possible was demonstrated in Israel with the Kibbutz program.

Foster homes and juvenile halls are not the answer. In many instances they have done more harm than good. Although some foster parents have done admirable jobs, the overall program has left much to be desired. Because small children are more often kept with their families, older ones are constituting an increasing proportion of the foster home populations. Many of them have emotional and behavioral problems to begin with and too often they experience neglect and abuse in the foster homes, and the teenage females are at special risk of early sexual activity and pregnancy.

Boarding schools would be where they could study and prepare themselves for careers, while in an environment that is helpful and nurturing, with expectations of responsibility and conforming behavior and morality and non-violence. They would learn consideration, experience rational supervision and be spared physical and sexual abuse.

Orphanages, group homes or asylums would provide similar environments for the younger children and could more easily be subjected to inspection and supervision than is now possible with foster home care.

There are those who claim that societies that have tried to substitute institutions for families have grown to regret the results. It may be that they are thinking of the orphan asylums of the past that provided environments devoid of warm human interaction with children.

For some single mothers whose parents are incapable of assuming their share of responsibility, who are incapable of working because of emotional or intellectual limitations, but can provide a warm caring upbringing for their children, financial assistance may be the best approach. Concern for the welfare of the illegitimate children deters society from punishing their mothers. Others may do well when given the alternative of working at home at jobs such as garment assembling or sewing while being with their children.

For working mothers with no other adult at home, after school programs for latch-key children are desperately needed. They could provide possibilities for recreation and sports, opportunity for assistance in homework, and special tutoring when needed. Supervisors, teachers or volunteers for this would be needed.

It is extremely important that psychopathology in children, easily identified in school, be recognized, and that appropriate steps be taken to deal with it and the family situation when and if it requires remedial action. Dysfunctional families will need help. Substance abusing or mentally ill parents will require assistance that now is so rarely available as a result of deinstitutionalization and reduced support for psychiatric facilities.

Employment, for those men and women who are able to work, should be as much a right as education and medical treatment. Work should be required of all who are able, by health and situations, to work—and reasonable compensation should be guaranteed. This, of course, will require planning, commitment and enforcement and some compromise with individual rights as they are now defined. Community work like picking up papers, cutting grass, being a watchman, cleaning up graffiti, etc., can be assigned if the person is unable to do anything requiring more skill.

The physically and mentally disabled will need help that is provided by the program for the totally disabled. Those who are temporarily out of work are eligible for Unemployment Compensation. Some will need help in finding a job, but the governmental employment agencies will continue to fail to assist many, in the absence of a plan for universal employment and a policy of denying welfare to the person who refuses to take a job he is capable of doing.

The Work Projects program (WPA) during the great depression in the 30s involved the creation of government jobs that, despite great criticism, helped many to get work that benefitted all of society.

There are many adolescents with antisocial personalities and histories of theft, violence and incorrigibility who will be the criminals and substance abusers as adults. Society is reluctant to confine them or (often) to even punish them. The criminal justice system has been unsuccessful in dealing with the problem. If they are in school, they disrupt classes, abuse teachers and other children, are often truant and often are relatively illiterate and uncivilized upon graduation. How much better off they (and society) would be if the Civilian Conservation Corps (the old CCC) were reactivated for the rehabilitation of these disordered kids who in almost every instance come from disturbed families. A structured, non-criminal environment away from gangs and ghettos helped many such young people in the past. They engaged in constructive environmental work, developed skills and adapted to some imposed discipline. They thrived in an environment free of drugs, violence, lawlessness, and pathogenic home situations. The CCC would provide the kind of change and some sanctuary for at risk children that was recommended by Franklyn Jenifer as the only resort in a society that ignores the need to eliminate detrimental environments.*

Neighborhood based urban voluntary residential schools, day schools and summer residential schools and camps are other alternatives that can be developed for children needing this kind of help.

What is being proposed is a multilevel set of facilities that could be employed appropriately for the many young people who otherwise are

---

*The Civilian Conservation Corps took 3 million young men off the street and put them to work on the land. They became innovators of the largest conservation corps and natural resource revitalization program in the history of the United States. During the nine years of its existence the CCC is credited with the development of more than 800 state parks, 4000 historical structures, 60,000 buildings and 38,500 bridges, untold miles of rustic rock and hand tools.

CCC workers built 97,000 miles of roads, 2470 fire towers, planted 4 billion trees, stocked 2 billion fish, arrested erosion of 200 million acres of land and fought fires and floods.

destined to become the self-defeating criminals and substance abusers we are now seeing.

Objections will quickly be raised because of the cost of such an approach. It costs about $30,000 to build each prison cell and approximately as much to house each prisoner each year. If the cost of the nation's criminal justice system with its courts, prisons, probation programs, drug programs, and help for the substance abusing, homeless, and mentally ill were ever determined, it would probably exceed by far the cost of a preventive program as outlined above.

A more responsive court system is required to be able to deal with child abuse and neglect in a more effective way than is now the case. With any sign of trouble, evaluation of the child and the home environment can be regarded as an opportunity to prevent a tragedy instead of a chore that will be unproductive. With genuine interest, ways of assisting dysfunctional families may be found. The problem is as urgent as the hole in the earth's stratospheric ozone layer. The consequences of ignoring it are as great.

Fathers should be required to contribute to the support of their children even if they have to do work they don't like or if it involves less for their second families. In California only 20 percent of parents who have been ordered to pay child support do so and the situation is no different in the rest of the country.

Men who fail to support, or neglect or abuse their children, and remain unresponsive to the usual efforts at corrective action, should be placed in correctional facilities with work programs for pay, not just confined. Their earnings can be used for the family, while the men are subjected to behavior therapy with the goal of improving their motivation and understanding. Those men who are responsive may not have to be confined, as long as they cooperate in providing support to the children they have fathered.

Existing welfare programs have been blamed for contributing to the creation of chronic dependency and the perpetuation of poverty with all of its negative consequences. While there is some justification for dissatisfaction with existing assistance programs, and their abuse, cutting out government welfare will not solve the many problems currently plaguing society, and may in fact, exaggerate them. There are, and in all likelihood, there will always be, some who will require help. But, there is reason to consider how and by whom and under what circumstances it is given.

Although many complain about the huge cost of welfare and other social services, even the most generous programs involve just a fraction of the people who are in need. Women receiving AFDC remain in poverty. Living conditions for many are deplorable, if existent. The homeless are still roaming the streets. Teenagers with babies and no husbands, struggle to survive. There are many men and women who want to work but can't find jobs. There are the retarded and the inept who are incapable of holding a job when given one and who will always need some help or supervision. There probably will never be enough money to take care adequately of all these problems. Clearly a different approach from the piece-meal attempted solutions of the past is needed. Attention must be directed to the causes of these perplexing societal dilemmas. Identifying the causes carries the promise of better treatment and the possibility of prevention.

The focus, thus far, has been on what can be done for children at risk. Direct treatment of the emotional, behavioral and cognitive problems of the children when given early is considered tertiary prevention to the extent that it keeps the problem from getting worse and offers the possibility of improvement. Likewise, treatment of the dysfunctional family, marital counseling, dealing with parental substance abuse and neglect, may also be regarded as preventive measures if they have a positive effect on the child. These approaches are not considered primary prevention and the topics will not be pursued here. They should, however, not be ignored.

In addition to the need to discourage teenage pregnancy, as a primary preventive measure, the problem of multiple births by incompetent, dysfunctional single women must be faced.

In a discussion of the problem of promiscuity and Public Health held at the University of Kentucky, the opinion was expressed that if good diet, not smoking, using seat belts and limiting alcohol intake are appropriate things for doctors to advise parents about, sexual behavior too should be included as it relates to health. It is irresponsible patients' behavior that places them at risk of contracting sexually transmitted diseases.

In a study of 7000 pregnant girls in San Antonio, many expressed the wish to have been told by someone that saying "no" to sexual activity was all right. Emphasizing the consequences of irresponsible sexual behavior in a New York study was found to be associated with less sexual activity then emphasizing contraception. Girls in the latter group were 34 percent more likely to be sexually active. One doctor pointed out that there would be no hesitation in informing people of the risk of life-threatening illnesses from a contaminated water supply, and that there should be no reluctance to warn about the risk of promiscuous sexual activity, and to point out that the only way to absolutely avoid the risk was to abstain from sexual activity. A condom does not offer complete protection. Many of the girls wanted someone to talk to them about their sexual conduct. They were confused by the conflicting messages they were getting from society. It may be that the religious requirement of a single sexual partner for life was adopted for its survival value and not just for a moral stance.[17]

Recently, a California judge attempted to force birth control on a single woman who was in jail for abusing her four children, three of whom were in foster homes. He made a surgical implantation of Norplant, which would prevent pregnancy for up to five years, a condition of her probation. His ruling was quickly challenged as unconstitutional—another example of the emphasis on human rights as opposed to the rights of society.[18]

The Governor of Wisconsin proposed capping funds for unmarried mothers at $440 a month and providing no increase if the woman has additional children, unless she gets married. Withholding benefits from families whose children cut class has also been recommended.

The preoccupation with individual rights has interfered with the development of a national approach to the problem of crime and substance abuse. Maintaining children in the home of a pathogenic biological parent has frequently seemed more important than providing a healthier alternative. For this to change, increased emphasis will have to be given to the rights of society and to the quality of life and stability in communities. The excessive promotion of individual rights and entitlements while neglecting any fostering of individual responsibility must give way to a more balanced social philosophy and compromise that will result in benefit for society as a whole.

Reducing the use of alcohol could help in the reduction of other substance abuse that so frequently follows. A higher tax on liquor may discourage its use as seems to be the case with tobacco.

A more responsive judicial system that is better able to deal with child abuse is essential. Without it the multifaceted approach to preventing substance abuse will not be possible.

Much of our societies' social problems is a reflection of abused children who disproportionately as adults engage in crime and substance abuse. If society is left unchanged, there is less likelihood of its solving the problems we are now so concerned about.

Danny Goldberg, Chair of the ACLU Foundation of Southern California and President of the Rock Against Drugs Foundation, maintains that, even if the drug cartels were crushed and cocaine miraculously wiped from the face of the earth, the alienation and lack of confidence in the future that have spawned drug gangs would still be there. Amphetamines, angel dust, alcohol, airplane glue—all sold here, would instantly replace cocaine if the misery of the underclass were not reduced.

"Only an America that gives every child a real stake in our future can produce the kind of social cohesion that will restore stability".[18] To achieve this, dysfunctional parents who underlie the psychopathology of children will have to be helped, and failing that, the young children taken away from them in order to have a chance for a constructive upbringing. In the long run, this would result in a reduced incidence of teenage pregnancies, substance abuse, crime and poverty.

Charles Krauthammer, the columnist, blames the message of instant gratification on modern advertising because he sees drug abuse as a form of instant gratification. He admits the vast majority of inner-city dwellers are not cocaine users—indicating that this is the idiosyncratic element in some individuals that predisposes the drug abuser—that it can in great part be traced to his early life experience.[19]

Appropriating money to fight the drug problem and provide treatment for the abusers may help but will not solve the problem. There is a limit to what can be accomplished by law enforcement and attempts to control behavior. More can be done by local communities, than is now done, to report drug dealers, violent gang members and other criminal activity. Residents of crime infested areas have a responsibility to assist in getting them cleaned up even if it means fewer boom boxes, gold chains and cars for the kids they know. If they want protection by the law, their attitudes toward law enforcement must change from an adversarial to a more cooperative one. The behavior of the police toward them should and probably would also improve.

To some extent there are cycles of substance abuse. New aberrations come about to replace the old. "Ice" may replace cocaine, as it replaced PCP and in turn, will probably be replaced by some equally frightening new concoction unless there are changes in society. Without these changes, we will continue to flounder with one or another ill-conceived solution as we have been doing with poverty and crime and other social problems.

William J. Bennett is of the opinion that the solution of the most pressing problem facing America (dissolution of the family, births to unwed mothers, Black on Black violence, low academic achievement, drop outs from school and the economy) rests in improvement in the criminal justice system, education, employment and social services, parental choice in education, accountability, merit pay, a solid core school curriculum, tenant ownership of public housing, affirmation of individual responsibility and the condemnation of irresponsible acts like out of wedlock births.[20] These are the goals that must be pursued.

Thomas Becker, Ph.D. of the Human Interaction Research Institute has stressed the power of the mass media to convey information, and provoke attitude change and sometimes behavior. Most Americans he says, get most of their knowledge about health issues from television.

Few health issues have received more attention in recent years than drug abuse and its prevention especially among young people. "If fighting substance abuse in the U.S. is dependent on resetting values, and refocusing attention, then mass media health behavior campaigns need to be designed in ways that take advantage of that reality."

The usual campaigns don't tend to reach the I.V. drug abusers—because of their social isolation and lifestyles and their psychological characteristics.

More effective campaigns address poverty and lack of economic opportunity that impinge on the problem. Effective campaigns for high risk youth may include specific educational messages to parents. Using peer models is more effective than celebrity adults—who are apt to be received with suspicion by youths who are rebellious against authority.

It is extremely difficult to determine if the mass media campaigns have had any beneficial influence so far. Kim Goldberg, Professor of Medicine in Dayton, Ohio points out that providing knowledge may not be sufficient to influence behavior. It is the person's values, interests, attitudes, feelings and culture that most influence his desire to change behavior.

George Bernard Shaw said, "The reasonable man adapts himself to the world; the unreasonable one persists in trying to adapt the world to himself. Therefore all progress depends on the unreasonable man." We need to be unreasonable if the drug (and its associated crime) problem is to be solved.

Goodwin, Director of the National Institute of Mental Health says, "Congress is paralyzed, passing deficit bills that won't affect the deficit and gun-control laws that won't control guns . . . class division is rapidly moving toward class war of the hopeless against the hopeless . . . The only hope is for a Jeffersonian revolution—a political movement outside the present party structure—that convinces people that it means business (in attacking crime, poverty and hopelessness)." "Leaders are afraid of all the unwelcome consequences that will follow advocacy of large changes in the direction of American life. In order to keep their positions as "leaders" they forfeit the right to lead." Goodwin who was a special assistant to Presidents Kennedy and Johnson urges "a movement with allegiance not to party but to principle, not to victory for politicians but to triumph for America. . . . not from the top but from the ascending pressure of a people distressed and angry at the loss of American greatness".[21]

Even if the public and politicians are unwilling to do what is necessary, physicians, and others who are faced with the consequences of substance abuse should continue to point out to the public Health Authorities what needs to be done. They should also be helping teenage girls from getting pregnant.

With the problems of crime, poverty, substance abuse and homelessness getting worse despite expenditures of huge sums money that were supposed to improve them, it seems clear that a different approach is needed. Since pathological childhood experiences appear to be a common factor in the origin of these societal problems, solutions should be based on preventing the trauma, neglect and abuse of children than give rise to the problems.

Societal attitudes will need to change. Exaggerated permissiveness will have to be replaced with a requirement that individuals be held responsible for what they do and parents for what their minor children do. Judgments about what is good and bad will have to be made. Violence in our homes, schools and communities cannot be tolerated. Discipline in schools must be enforced and rewards for failure stopped. Vocational training should be provided for students who are not academically oriented. It should be recognized that college is not appropriate for all students.

Irresponsible individuals must be discouraged from having children and parents who are incapable of rearing children to become productive adults will have to give them up.

Broken windows that are not fixed, graffiti that is not removed, drunks and homeless who are permitted to lie in the streets, all point to lack of concern that people have about their environment and according to James Q. Wilson's *Theory of Social Decay,* there will follow vandalism and progressive deterioration of the neighborhood. It is crucial to fight over minor infractions if a neighborhood is to be saved. This would entail an end to the emphasis on individual rights and uncalled for compassion and a better balance between the rights of the community and the rights of the individual.[22]

It is likely that society will not be willing to do what is necessary in which case it is unlikely that the drug, crime, poverty and welfare problems will be solved. However, it should not keep concerned persons from saying what should be done. It may prevent the development and implementation of expensive programs that are doomed to fail. Treatment programs clearly have not been successful in eliminating the problem. A majority of potential social failures can be identified early in life and the best solution will depend on prevention.

Lest we rely too much on the actions of government, we should heed the words of John Lubbock (1834–1913), an English naturalist, banker, and politician, and a member of Parliament where he promoted measures regulating hours of work and establishing libraries and parks: "It is important as far as possible, not so much to give a man bread, as to put him in the way of earning it for himself, not to give direct aid, but to help others to help themselves. The world is so complex that we must all inevitably owe much to our neighbors, but, as far as possible, every man should stand on his own feet. We must be careful not to undermine independence in our anxiety to relieve distress. There is always the initial difficulty, that whatever is done for man takes away from him a great stimulus to work and weakens the feeling of independence; all creatures which depend on others tend to become mere parasites." Lubbock said it was astonishing to see how many great men have been poor.

REFERENCES

1. *U.S. Medicine,* Jan. 1, 1977; p. 2.
2. Cockburn, A.: *L.A. Times,* Feb. 23, 1992; p. M5.
3. *The Western Journal of Medicine,* April 1976; 124:4, p. 329.
4. Wilson, J.Q., *UCLA Emeritus Newsletter,* Spring 1192; vol. 5. no. 3.
5. What Should We Do About The Poor? *Wall Street Journal,* April 14, 1992; p. A18.

6. Thomas, C.: *L.A. Times,* Nov. 11, 1991; p. B5.

7. Vatz, R. & Weinberg, L.: The Indulgence Epidemic. *L.A. Times,* Aug. 11, 1985; Part IV. p. 5.

8. Kort, M.: A Story Well Told. *UCLA Magazine,* Fall 1991; p. 31.

9. Tifft, S.: Who's Teaching Our Children? *Time,* Nov. 4, 1988; p. 58.

10. Fund, J.H.: Milwaukee's Schools Open—to Competition. *Wall Street Journal,* Sept. 4, 1990; p. A10.

11. Leo, J.: The Sorry Teaching of Teachers. *U.S. News & World Report,* April 27, 1992; p. 28.

12. Thomas, C.: Must Adolescents Submit To The Chain Saw Of Sex Education in the Public Schools? *L.A. Times,* Apr. 27, 1990; Part II. p. 7.

13. Raspberry, W.: L.A. Times, May 22, 1990; p. B7.

14. Antonio, M.: Tough Medicine for a Sick America. *L.A. Times,* Mar. 22, 1992; p. 32.

15. Kinsley, M.: *Time,* May 15, 1992; p. 90.

16. Leo, J.: The Hollowing of America. *Time,* Dec. 20, 1992; p. 85.

17. Abbott, S.: Medical Ethics Grand Rounds. *Hosp. Practice,* September 15, 1990; p. 63.

18. *L.A. Times,* January 17, 1991; p. B6.

19. *L.A. Times,* September 10, 1989, p. 5.

20. Editorial, *Wall Street Journal,* April 1, 1991.

21. *L.A. Times,* May 16, 1991 p. B7 and March 19, 1991, p. B5.

22. Leo, J.: Fighting For Our Public Spaces. *U.S. News & World Report,* February 3, 1992; p. 18.